The Great Dictators

Interviews with Filmmakers of Italian Descent

ESSAY SERIES 42

Guernica Editions Inc. acknowledges the support of the Canada Council for the Arts.

Canadä

Guernica Editions Inc. acknowledges the financial support of the Government of Canada through the Book Publishing Industry Development Program (BPIDP).

ANGELA BALDASSARRE

THE GREAT DICTATORS

INTERVIEWS WITH FILMMAKERS OF ITALIAN DESCENT

GUERNICA
TORONTO·BUFFALO·LANCASTER (U.K.)
1999

Copyright © 1999 by Angela Baldassarre
and Guernica Editions Inc.
All rights reserved. The use of any part of this publication,
reproduced, transmitted in any form or by any means,
electronic, mechanical, photocopying, recording or otherwise
stored in a retrieval system, without the prior consent of the
publisher is an infringement of the copyright law.

Antonio D'Alfonso, editor
Guernica Editions Inc.
P.O. Box 117, Station P, Toronto (ON), Canada M5S 2S6
2250 Military Road, Tonawanda, N.Y., 14150-6000 U.S.A.
Gazelle, Falcon House, Queen Square, Lancaster LA1 1RN U.K.

Printed in Canada.
Legal Deposit — First Quarter
National Library of Canada
Library of Congress Card Number: 99-61707
Canadian Cataloguing in Publication Data
Baldassarre, Angela
The great dictators :
interviews with filmmakers of Italian descent
(Essay series ; 42)
ISBN 1-55071-094-X
1. Motion picture producers and directors — Italy —Interviews.
2. Motion picture producers and directors
— United States — Interviews.
I. Title. II. Series : Essay series (Toronto, Ont.) ; 42.
PN1998.2.B33 1999 791.43'023'0000922 C99-900377-1

Contents

Gianni Amelio Talks About *Lamerica*   7
Dario Argento Talks About *The Stendhal Syndrome*   12
Roberto Benigni Talks About *La vita è bella*   16
Bernardo Bertolucci Talks About *Little Buddha*   22
Bernardo Bertolucci Talks About *Stealing Beauty*   27
Franco Brusati Talks About *The Sleazy Uncle*   34
Steve Buscemi Talks About *Trees Lounge*   37
Tom DiCillo Talks About *Box of Moonlight*   42
Mimmo Calopresti Talks About *La Seconda Volta*   45
Michael Corrente Talks About *American Buffalo*   49
Don Coscarelli Talks About *Phantasm*   54
Richard LaGravanese Talks About *Living Out Loud*   57
Anthony Minghella Talks About *The English Patient*   62
Nanni Moretti Talks About His Career   66
Greg Mottola Talks About *The Daytrippers*   72
Maurizio Nichetti Talks About *Luna e l'altra*   76
Al Pacino Talks About *Looking for Richard*   79
Leone Pompucci Talks About *Mille Bolle Blue*   86
Gabriele Salvatores Talks About *Mediterraneo*   89
Michele Soavi Talks About *Dellamorte Dellamore*   93
Giuseppe Tornatore Talks About *Everybody's Fine*   96
Stanley Tucci Talks About *Big Night*   101

For Alessandro

Gianni Amelio
Talks About *Lamerica*

Italian director Gianni Amelio has a technique that typifies his restrained approach to issues affecting his beloved country. With his extraordinary first feature, *Colpire al cuore* (*Blow to the Heart,* 1982), the director has the subject of terrorism hovering over the picture like a miasma, but refuses to explore it. Instead he's more concerned with family relationships and examining the consequences on an only child of parents who keep themselves at a distant.

With the Oscar-nominated *Porte Aperte (Open Doors)*, although the film's first few minutes show three brutal murders and a rape, Amelio has little interest in tackling the obvious, and bigger themes of Fascism and the death penalty head on. Instead, he subtly concentrates on the character of the tolerant judge (Gian Maria Volonté) and the failing compassion of the period. The same goes for *Il Ladro di Bambini (Stolen Children),* where the initial premise seems to be the plight of two abused children, but quickly turns into an indictment of a seriously failing Italy with its ruined environment and degraded human relations.

No film, in fact, deals with the Italians too frequent moments of shame than *Lamerica,* Amelio's latest and most ambitious picture. Like his other movies, here the director subtly explores the powerful forces that control our lives by critically uncovering the guilt that accompanies most of our actions.

"I believe it's very difficult to admit to your faults," says the fifty-year-old director who was in Toronto recently to promote the movie. "We Italians have so many of them but we always seem to find a justification. This is a typical Italian vice. In *Il Ladro di bambini*, for example, there are so many illegalities happening to the poor children, yet everyone is saying that laws are meant to be broken. The same happens in *Lamerica*. We have to rid our lives of this vice because every time we commit a criminal act, someone else suffers the consequences. This duo reality is evident in all my films. There's someone who commits the violence and some who's the recipient of it."

Lamerica tells the story of two Italian businessmen (Michele Placido and Enrico Lo Verso) who go to newly-democratic Albania with the intent of buying a factory by adopting the help of a corrupt government official. Regulations, however, require they take on an Albanian figurehead partner to comply with the privatization laws. They find such a person in an elderly political prisoner just released from jail who in turn leads the youngest of the Italians on a journey of self-discovery.

"*Lamerica* is my most personal film," admits Amelio. "It deals with a theme that is very close to my heart: emigration. My father and grandfather were emigrants, so were most of my family. Almost the entire town I grew up in emptied out in the 1950s. I remained in the region of Calabria by pure chance with my mother and sister, and stayed until I moved to

Rome as an adult. The lucky ones emigrated to North America. The unfortunates, like my father, went to Argentina where he remained for fifteen years. When I saw the telecast showing thousands of Albanians fleeing to Italy with their hungry faces, I saw the faces of my father, my uncles, my entire family. Calabria of the 1950s was as poor as Albania is today. I saw in the Albanians my family's history."

As with all his films, Amelio forces the young protagonist of *Lamerica* to undergo a catharsis that reflects the growing apathy of Italy's youth with regards to their country's past.

"This is the most important aspect of the film, this path that leads him to change for the better," explains Amelio. "He's an extremely arrogant, egotistical person who goes to Albania with all this negative baggage. He has no idea of what Italy's past was; what kind of country Italy was before the affluent period he's living in. I force him to undergo the same suffering as the Albanians; I force him to travel through the poorest parts of Albania's interior just so he can understand what famine means. This is probably the only way for him to relate to others."

What of Amelio, then? Having filmed in impoverished Albania with local non-actors, did the director also undergo some form of catharsis?

"I had no need," he smiles. "When I went to Albania it felt like returning to the home of my childhood. I've experienced misery, poverty...I'm very familiar with Italy of that period. That's why I love the Albanians the way I do, because they resemble Italians so much."

In the past decade Amelio has emerged as arguably the most important filmmaker working in Europe today by reviving neorealism with his compassionate vision of modern-day conflicts. This is a comparison that the filmmaker encourages explaining that only by adopting the old masters' techniques is he able to credibly stress the symbolic importance of the accusations he displays in his pictures.

"De Sica and Zavattini felt that only by using real-life personages rather than professional actors could the focal point of a theme be plausibly expressed," says Amelio. "That's why I choose Carmelo Di Mazzarelli to play the elderly Albanian. I took a great risk casting him. I began searching for someone like him in Sicily because the character had to be a southerner. I was in Marina di Ragusa, where I filmed a huge chunk of *Ladro di Bambini,* and on the first day I met this man who had the most expressive eyes. He was very gaunt, small, minute, he was of great intelligence... He was the character I had envisioned. But I had to work hard with him. It was worth it. When he got a standing ovation at the Venice film festival two years ago, he broke down in tears. He told me that he never expected that, at this point in his life, someone could bless him with such a gift."

Filmography

Gianni Amelio was born on 20 January 1945, in San Pietro Magisano, Catanzaro, Italy.

Così ridevano (1998)
Lamerica (1994)
Il Ladro di bambini (1992)
Porte aperte (1990)
I Ragazzi di via Panisperna (1988)
6 Mina (1985)
Camera oscura (1985)
La Squadra del lunedì (1985)
Idalina (1984)
Passeggeri (1984)
Vocazione (1984)
I Velieri (1983)
Colpire al cuore (1982)
Il piccolo Archimede (1979)
Effetti speciali (1978)
La Morte al lavoro (1978)
Bertolucci secondo il cinema (1975)
La Città del sole (1973)
La Fine del gioco (1970)
Il Campione (1967)
Undici immigranti (1967)

Dario Argento
Talks About *The Stendhal Syndrome*

Since directing his first film, *The Bird with the Crystal Plumage* (1969), Dario Argento has been hailed as Italy's horror-meister and one of the most original genre moviemakers of our time because of his ornate visual style that celebrates striking imagery and idiosyncratic use of colour over plot and structure. *Deep Red* (1975), *Suspiria* (1977), *Inferno* (1980), and *Creepers* (1984) and *Trauma* (1992), made almost a decade later, reveal a mastery of visual technique although Argento's disturbing visions and sadistic flirtations make these works tough going for mainstream viewers.

Following a three-year hiatus from directing his American film, *Trauma,* which was poorly received, Argento has decided to return to his native Italy to make *The Stendhal Syndrome,* a psychological drama starring his daughter, and rising star, Asia, which is premiering at the Toronto International Film Festival this week.

"Because I made two films in the U.S. [the other being *Two Evil Eyes* (1991)], I wanted to return to Italy to make a real Italian movie," explains Argento from his home in Rome. "That's why I filmed in the Uffizi Gallery, in medieval cities like Viterbo, and the most beautiful streets of Rome. I wanted to make a high-concept European movie."

And that he did beautifully. *The Stendhal Syndrome,* in fact, opens in Florence's Uffizi Gallery where a woman is so transfixed by artwork that it thrusts her into a hallucinatory trance. At one point she falls into painting, Rembrandt's *Nightwatch,* where she discovers that her true identity is that of a policewoman investigating a series of gruesome murders.

"Many years ago I read a book called *The Stendhal Syndrome,* explains Argento. "It was based on research done on perturbations caused by artwork. This is an ancient condition, but it never had a name before. I then remembered an incident when I was a child visiting Greece with my parents and I became very ill in front of the Parthenon. I eventually realized that I was suffering from the same syndrome."

The Stendhal Syndrome, in fact, affects some people who are in certain cities where certain types of art, particularly from the Renaissance period, will have them experience illnesses such as nausea, fainting spells and, at times, personality splits.

"Often one thinks of artwork as something that generates an euphoric feeling, a happy feeling," says Argento. "But sometimes masterpieces can cause great emotional commotion. I wanted to tell a story of how works of great art can perturb a person so much that it would make her personality so fragile to make it split. It's so strange that art can provoke a catharsis so strong."

Indeed. Even while filming *The Stendhal Syndrome,* the only movie ever to be filmed in the Uffizi

Gallery, Argento had to overcome enourmous emotional turmoil.

"It was an amazing experience," he remembers. "Usually there a thousands of people lining up for hours waiting to see these works, and here I was for days on end with these masterpieces at my fingertips. I would walk around the corridors at night, looking at Da Vinci's and Rembrandt's in deserted rooms, in the dark with this incredibly exhilarating but scary feeling. I could feel the presence of the artists around me, so strong are their works. There were nights where I could swear they appeared in front of me. It was the most amazing experience."

FILMOGRAPHY

Dario Argento was born on 7 September 1940, in Rome, Italy.

Phantom of the Opera (1998)
La Sindrome di Stendhal (1996)
... aka *The Stendhal Syndrome* (1996)
... aka *Stendhal's Syndrome* (1996)
Trauma (1992)
... aka *Aura's Enigma* (1992)
... aka *Dario Argento's Trauma* (1992)
Two Evil Eyes (1990)
... aka *Due occhi diabolici* (1990)
... aka *Edgar Allan Poe* (1989)
Opera (1987)
... aka *Terror at the Opera* (1987)
Phenomena (1984)
... aka *Creepers* (1984)
Tenebre (1982)
... aka *Shadow* (1982)
... aka *Sotto gli occhi dell'assassino* (1982)
... aka *Tenebrae* (1982)
... aka *Unsane* (1982)
Inferno (1980)

... aka *Dario Argento's Inferno* (1980)
Suspiria (1977)
... aka *Dario Argento's Suspiria* (1977)
Profondo rosso (1975)
... aka *Deep Red* (1975)
... aka *Deep Red Hatchet Murders* (1975)
... aka *Dripping Deep Red* (1975)
... aka *The Hatchet Murders* (1975)
... aka *The Sabre Tooth Tiger* (1975)
... aka *Suspiria 2* (1975)
Le Cinque giornate (1973)
... aka *The Five Days of Milan* (1973)
Testimone oculare (TV, 1972, as Roberto Pariente)
Il Tram (TV, 1972, as Sirio Bernadotte)
4 mosche di velluto grigio (1971)
... aka *Four Flies on Grey Velvet* (1971)
... aka *Four Patches of Grey Velvet* (1971)
Il Gatto a nove code (1970)
... aka *The Cat o' Nine Tails* (1970)
L'Uccello dalle piume di cristallo (1969)
... aka *The Bird with the Crystal Plumage* (1969)
... aka *Bird with the Glass Feathers* (1969)
... aka *The Gallery Murders* (1969)
... aka *Das Geheimnis der schwarzen Handschuhe* (1969)
... aka *Phantom of Terror* (1969)

Roberto Benigni
Talks About *Life Is Beautiful*

Roberto Benigni is that rare Italian phenomenon: a little whirlwind of comic genius combined with the right dose of intellect and humanity. His latest film, *La vita è bella*, has won accolades worldwide because of its wonderful premise: a Jewish man protects his young son from the horrors of a Nazi concentration camp by playing a game of make-believe. Irresistible, poignant and memorable... like its director/star.

Why is life beautiful for you?

What a beautiful question. It's wonderful to be alive, even when doesn't think so. I'm convinced that the real life, that which contains a clear and healthy mind, and when we're not prone to mysticisms or extreme enthusiasms, the normal life, the one where one suffers, that's real life. That gives me immense satisfaction. That gives me the will to live. Without those moments of sadness we wouldn't appreciate the beauty of life. I love having those sad moments because I like to experience every emotion that life has given me, not only those happy ones. I also think it's important not to have huge ideologies. They're dangerous. I think life is beautiful when there's no need to achieve such huge goals. Then we can dedicate our time to relationships with people. That I think is beautiful.

Unfortunately, most of the time those are the issues that put on the back burner.

What inspired you to make La Vita è bella?

Another beautiful but difficult question because one never knows where the inspiration comes from. In fact, I don't know where the inspiration came for any of my films. But there was a time when I felt a huge desire, a profound desire, to put myself, as a comedian, in an extreme situation that also featured a love story. I was in the mood to make a beautiful love story. Then I thought of what is the most extreme situation, the most horrendous historical moment of our existence, and that was the Second World War. At the beginning I thought of it as a paradox, then I wondered why I was afraid.

Afraid of what?

Well, there's a hang-up about a comedian making a movie about concentration camps. Not a comedy film about concentration camps, but a comedian making a movie about concentration camps. But I was honest with myself. When I thought of the idea about a child and making him believe that nothing was real, that everything was a game set during history's greatest horror, I felt like I was telling myself that as well. That I was telling myself that it didn't happen, that I didn't want to believe it, that it wasn't possible, not true. It's the same reaction that the survivors had immediately after being released. Primo Levi wrote about it in his books. He wrote the first reaction was so terrifying, that he thought it was all some elaborate joke, a nightmare from which they would wake up. That's what they were at least hoping. Once they found out what had truly happened, then they had this great need to talk about it.

Is that what you're doing with film? Talking about it?

Yes. I felt the need to do something about it because once one finds out about, reads about the holocaust, one is no longer the same person. That happened to me; I changed after I read about what happened. One doesn't need to be Jewish be affected by it.

Your father was also in a concentration camp during the war.

Yes, but my father isn't Jewish; he was a prisoner of war who was sent to a labour camp where the conditions were similar to those of concentration camps but without the gas chambers. That made a huge difference. When he returned home he weighed 34 kilos; he was a skeleton of himself.

Why was he imprisoned?

On the 8th of September the American allies landed in Sicily, and the Italian government, led by Badoglio, broke with the Germans so the Italian suddenly were enemies of the Germans. My father, who knew nothing because he was just a farmer fighting a war he knew nothing about, was in Albania with other soldiers and was suddenly taken prisoner by the Germans. He was imprisoned in a labour camp in Germany for two years and nearly everyone from his battalion died. Only seven or eight prisoners survived. It then took my father two months to reach Arezzo from Germany following the liberation, just like Primo Levi tells in *La Tregua*. He returned home obsessed by this experience and he had this need to tell the story every day in order for people, and himself, to understand what happened.

So you know the story by heart.

Of course. Myself and my three sisters listened to him incessantly. Anything would spark the conversation, a piece of bread, some water. He would talk about insects crawling over dead bodies, of unimaginable horrors, of diseases. He had nightmares, every night the same dream about boarding a train and telling those in the train everything that happened to him. It was very painful listening to him. Then one day, after years of me and my sisters hearing the same stories, my father began the tale and we just finished the sentence for him. He broke into a smile. Then he began telling us the story with humour put in, in order not to traumatize us. He began to laugh and from that moment on he was freed of the nightmares. He never hated anyone or anything, and he never blamed anyone for what happened to him. I was always very touched by this. My sisters and I laughed often at how he would recite these tragedies.

Are some of his stories in your film?

No. None of them but the atmosphere is there, the manner in which he told us those stories in order to protect us from the horrors, that's how I talk to the child in the film. My father is a very funny man, he loves life, he's full of life, he loves making love, he's a beautiful example of a father, very pure. He helped me a lot in making this film. He was very taken by the way I approached this movie.

Did you ever think of changing the ending to the movie?

Yes, but it's dangerous. If in the end the entire family gets back together and smile, it would be disrespectful. I can fool around all I want in the concentration camp, but in the end I have to suffer the consequences, realistically. But I live through my son who is healthy, who has suffered no trauma, who is human and pure. For me to protect his innocence was the most important and precious thing. It's instinctive in all of us to protect our children at the cost of our lives. The distributors wanted a different ending in order to attract children to the film, but I felt that children can handle death. They understand the rapport between life and death. They find it normal.

Are you surprised at the film's international success?

Yes, and I'm also very happy about because it's a sign of love. A comedian is dead without the love of his audience. One can watch a tragic film on his own, but a comedy without an audience, without the laughter, the emotions, is lost. I'm surprised but also very happy because it's a manifestation of love which I wholeheartedly accept and return.

FILMOGRAPHY

Roberto Benigni was born in Misericordia, Arezzo, Italy, on 27 October 1952.

La vita è bella (*Life Is Beautiful,* 1997)
Il Mostro (The Monster, 1994)
Johnny Stecchino (Johnny Toothpick, 1991)
Il piccolo diavolo (The Little Devil, 1988)
Non ci resta che piangere (Nothing Left to Do But Cry, 1984)

Tu mi turbi (1983)

Actor

Asterix et Obélix contre César (1999)
La vita è bella (1997)
Il mostro (1994)
Son of the Pink Panther (1993)
Night on Earth (1991)
Johnny Stecchino (1991)
La Voce della luna (1989)
Il piccolo diavolo (1988)
Down By Law (1986)
Coffee and Cigarettes (1986)
Non ci resta che piangere (1984)
F.F.S.S. Cioè che mi hai portato a fare sopra Posillipo se non mi vuoi più bene (1983)

Bernardo Bertolucci Talks About *Little Buddha*

Few of us ever get the opportunity to meet a childhood idol. Not that I was exactly a child when I first discovered Bernardo Bertolucci, but at thirteen, having gone to see *The Conformist* with my junior-high class in Italy, I felt that I was being reborn into a new world. A world not just of images and sounds — which are typical of most films I'd seen until then — but of astounding thoughts and passion.

I decided then that if Luchino Visconti were to die, Bertolucci would take his place as my favourite director. Visconti died in 1976, and by then I had seen some of Bertolucci's past films *(Before the Revolution, The Spider's Stratagem)* and his new ones *(Last Tango in Paris* and *1900* which is my favourite film of all time). To this day he remains at the top of my list although his last few films do not.

Since leaving Italy's claustrophobic movie industry, Bertolucci has directed an Academy Award-winner *(The Last Emperor)*, an essay on Westerners in the East *(The Sheltering Sky)* and a step-by-step guide to understanding Buddhism *(Little Buddha)*.

Here are some of his thoughts.

What sparked your interest in Buddhism?

I was fascinated by several books I had read. I learned how to meditate, still I didn't know anything about Buddhism. Then in 1989, after I had done *The Sheltering Sky,* there was a moment where I couldn't hold my beliefs anymore, my beliefs of a utopical society. Buddhism gave me the courage to go on with something else. Our culture, which is the culture of the West, has become such a global culture, unique culture, that it's become a huge, mystical umbrella of the world where all other cultures disappear. In fact, to do *The Last Emperor,* also to do *The Sheltering Sky,* and to do *Little Buddha,* was my way of helping people to discover cultures they didn't know before.

Do you believe in reincarnation?

The Tibetan idea of reincarnation with Lamas going around the world looking for children who are possibly the reincarnations of their gurus, masters, teachers, is a beautiful idea. I don't think that I can believe like a Tibetan that you can find a reincarnate which has a name, an address and a phone number. But I respect and I like the idea of reincarnation because it's a metaphor for Tibetans to keep surviving their culture. I think there is reincarnation of ideas. In fact, I think we are reincarnated all our lives. There was a poem by Borges, the Argentinean writer who was very, very fascinated by Buddhism, that says 'The fish lives in the ocean and the man remembers he once was that fish.' It's a poetic idea about reincarnation. Another thing: children — and this movie has been done also for children because children have been kept away from my movies. We did a preview for children in Jersey, and what came out in the end was interesting. Today children are afraid of death. This is something completely new. When I was a child I thought I was immortal. Today children, because of the news, children dying in Sarajevo and Somalia, they've discovered that they can die and they are very, very upset. The idea of reincarnation makes them ecstatic, absolutely excited about the idea of coming back.

The film is set in ancient India. You cast all Indian actors for the roles except for Keanu Reeves who plays Prince Siddhartha. Why?

I'm always trying to go for the real thing. They are all Tibetan monks and Lamas in the film, except for Ying Ruocheng who plays Lama Norbu, who is a Chinese actor. All the others are the real thing. I had this English casting director who spent more than two months in India sending me hundreds of tapes for the role. It was very difficult to find among these actors the right Siddhartha. I was really desperate, and I read somewhere that Keanu Reeves was half-American, half-Canadian, and half-Hawaiian-Chinese, and I said. "Let's meet him, let's see how he is." I've only seen him in one movie which I really liked very, very much called *My Own Idaho*. Keanu had a shining innocence on his face which he will have all his life. Whatever he does, whatever kind of perversion he has, he portrays this wonderful innocence. I knew that some moralists, some purists would be outraged. But I went for him because I really liked him and I thought he looked right. I like the result. I think he's charming, enchanting. He couldn't have done the preaching Buddha, though, but for the prince that one day will wake up, he was fine.

Why did you decide to use an American child as a reincarnate instead of one from another Western culture?

There is a Spanish child and another kid in France who are reincarnates. Since we have this confrontation between the past and the present all the time, I thought it was very important to have a very, very strong contrast. I was looking for a very modern landscape, an urban landscape. So we looked in America. Seattle was the city which seemed the most progressive. I was looking for a very modern city very far away from these spiritual ideas. I wanted the audience to be able to identify with the mother and the father. The mother is quite open, the father is quite skeptical, but they're not so closed that every time someone knocks at the door they open with a gun.

Why cast singer Chris Isaak as the father?

For the father and the mother I wanted a mother who was immediately open, more open, smarter somehow. For the father I wanted the kind of all-American, solid, physically strong man with materialistic motives. I wanted, at the end of the film, to add a new light in his face, another expression. Instead of going for a well-known actor, I'd rather go with somebody new. I don't see a lot of MTV so I didn't know who Chris Isaak was. He has this quality of honesty and strength.

Did the Dalai Lama see the film?

He saw it in Paris. He was one of the first people we showed it to. He told us something that was very amusing before the movie began. He said, "This is the first time I've entered a movie theatre." So I sat next to him through the film, and I was looking at him to observe the cinema initiation of such a great man.

What did he say about film?

First he said, "It's so very, very big." Then, a few times, he took my hands and held them. He laughed out loud when he recognized many of the Lamas.

Why did you film three movies in the Orient?

Because I was fed up with the Italian society in the 1980s. Economically, it was going through a boom, but, let me tell you, the smell of corruption was making it very difficult for me to feel inspired to do a movie about Italian society. I felt like going away as far as possible, and I went to China to make *The Last Emperor*. I wanted to feel free to film a society that is not just about consumerism. After *Little Buddha* I spent two months promoting the film and Italy seemed to be changing for the better. But after the elections in March, for the first time the right wing has won the elections as a majority since Mussolini. I think it's quite embarrassing. We are the only government with fascists who have seats in the government. I think there is a lack of historical memory in Italy. Young people don't remember anything. That's why one day I'd like to go back and do a third part to my movie *1900*, from 1945 to nowadays, just to remind people what went on.

Bernardo Bertolucci Talks About *Stealing Beauty*

As one of Italy's last surviving master filmmakers — if not the world — Bernardo Bertolucci has been elusive when talking about his next projects, and often waiting years between films. Following a fifteen-year hiatus from filming in Italy, Bertolucci has returned to his beloved country to make *Stealing Beauty,* an intimate tale about a nineteen-year-old American girl, Lucy (Liv Tyler) who visits British family friends in Tuscany in the hopes of rekindling a childhood love.

Why make a movie of this kind after so many "epics"?

After ten years it was starting to be a bit too much. Ten years of very big scale. Also, I was becoming very, very ambitious. The last ambitious thing was *Little Buddha,* and I didn't think I could go much farther than that. Also, the desire to change because if you look back to my movies, which are not too many, you would see that there's always kind of a decision not to repeat myself. I'm very obsessed with the fear of repeating myself because I see so many directors that I admire who, at a certain moment in their lives, start to repeat themselves and do the same thing. When you see from *Last Tango in Paris,* which is so intimate, I do *1900,* and people told me, "Why don't you do another *Last Tango in Paris?* Then I do *Luna,* which is about a mother and son... so there's always a desire to escape the demon of repetition.

Why film in Italy after fifteen years?

A desire to go back to my country, simply. I was homesick on one hand; on the other hand the conditions in the country, the conditions that sent me away in the 1980s which was when I found that Italy had become so corrupted that I didn't really have any desire to shoot there have changed. Now we have a country that's trying to change, that's doing a big trial about corruption, which, by the way, proves that I wasn't wrong when I left. It was a good moment to go back. Meanwhile, I'd been away so long that I didn't feel like doing immediately a film about Italian reality which I could be wrong about. So I said let's first go back with a kind of foreigner position. You think of Italy's beauty, especially, the beauty of the landscape. Also, I had the feeling that a completely new phase was starting. The first person who understood that was my father, who's eighty-five, and a poet, and who saw the film and with a smile said, "Bravo, il tuo primo film" ("Your first film"). I said, "You didn't like nothing so far?" and he said, "No, I love your movies but this is to me like something where you start again." And maybe that's why I decided to do a movie about a young girl who is looking for herself; maybe I wanted really to start again, to start from the beginning.

How was the film received in Italy?

A big big hit. It has a kind of fantastic box office. We did more than *Toy Story*.

Were you worried about some resentment from the Italian journalists?

I was a little bit nervous about what the Italian journalists might say, like "Why do you come back and talk about a group of expatriates from England?" But no one said that. They looked at the film and there was almost a kind of unanimous good feeling. But it was one of my movies that went better in Italy.

When you cast Liv Tyler? Did you know she had similar background to Lucy?

I found out after I met her. I was very excited about meeting her. I was very sure that at the end she would be the one. I asked her a month later to come to London to do a test with Jeremy Irons. They would the play the scene where they first meet at night and they smoke a joint and she she notices how sick he is. She comes to London and I give her the screenplay. She reads it and comes to the test, and says, "It's amazing, it's my story." I asked, "What?" "Yeah. Like Lucy I was adopted. Only when I was ten years old did I find out that my father was Steve Tyler." I think this gave her a kind of familiarity with the story. I think that the moment when this element of familiarity helped was when Donal McCann, the sculptor, and Liv have the meeting at the end when there's a kind of recognition between the father and the daughter. Nothing is said. It's just on the emotional side. At that moment her private story found a new meaning, and it showed in her acting.

What did she bring to the film?

First of all, and I'm trying to be simple, there was a mixture of innocence and sensuality which is very important for the character. And then that thing, which I saw the first time I met her, which is a girl who can move constantly between ages. I couldn't tell how old she was when I met her, I couldn't really because it was twenty minutes, very fast, and she was seventeen, but then she was thirteen. She looked at me when I asked her a question and she seemed a thirteen-year old, but then she turned around she became twenty-five, very fatale. This moving between different ages is really something which seduced me about her. I thought to myself that if I'm able to catch this change with a camera, than the viewe will see it in the film. When she's with Daisy, the little girl, she becomes a little girl too. Then, when she's with the grown-ups, she's a grown-up. It's something that gives a sense of the real thing, giving reality and truth to the character. That is what she brings. She brings an extraordinary unique sense of cinema. I mean, her relationship with the camera is something which I've rarely seen before. There's a kind of seduction between the camera and Liv, they're seducing each other, it's like a ballet. It's very strange. It's something that comes from a natural gift, because she didn't study acting.

Do you think that actors can lie on camera?

I think that when they lie it shows up. The fact is that actors are able to be what they're not without lying when they're good actors. This is a big discussion I had with Marlon Brando when we were making *Last Tango in Paris* because I was going on saying, "I want to take off your mask. I don't want your mask. I've seen it many times. I want you." When we met two years ago, I asked Brando, "Twenty years later do you think that I failed or succeeded in taking off the actor's studio mask?" He looked at me with a little smile and said, "Do you think that that one was me?" He laughed.

What attracted you to Liv Tyler?

In American tradition of literature, like in Henry James, these girls are kind of carriers of the American strength, something which is really connected with the nature of this country and the people of this country. They go to Europe and they find that they are vulnerable. They find themselves very fragile, so together the strength and the vulnerability of Liv were very captivating.

In what sense do you identify with Lucy?

I have to identify with all my characters otherwise it doesn't work. I had to be a Chinese emperor at a certain point.

Lucy's a poet and your father's a poet. Was there a connection?

I asked writer Susan Minot to push on the mother figure as a poet because my father is a poet and when I was a teenager I was a poet. I was writing a lot of poems and that helped me to get in Lucy's shoes. That's why she writes poems in the film. I even decided to have the poem written on the screen, even though it was childish and sweet. Flaubert said, *"Madame Bovary, c'est moi."* I asked Susan to write the film because Lucy's a girl and I wanted a woman writer. Lucy is an American girl so I wanted an American woman writer. I read her Monkeys in the 1980s and I liked it very much, so I thought she would be right. Then I was pushing hard to create for myself as many occasions of identification as possibe. I also found out that Susan Minot was secretly a poet, and so I pushed that. There's a moment, a kind of unveiling of the story of the father which is not the father, that she was conceived in the olive grove, it's a poem that Susan had written.

Does your father acknowledge his influence?

My father is so much of poet that he takes it for granted, so much so that for him everything that comes from him is poetry. I come from him and so I'm part of his poetry. It's what he taught me in life: to see poetry in everything like in daily life.

Did this film in some way prepare you for the next one which is about the 1960s?

It has been in the sense that it gave me the chance to spend as much time with kids today. Like Liv and her friends who came on the set to see her. To speak with them and to realize that there is this extraordinary amnesia in their memory about the recent past. And that I found very stimulating in trying to unveil that moment in 1968, a moment everywhere in the world when there was an explosion for young people.

You appeared in the film Un delitto italiano *about Pier Paolo Pasolini's murder. How did that reopen your feelings of that period?*

When I saw the film and saw myself in the film, the film gave me was the feeling of immense loss, a loss that nothing was able to refill. There is no chance that the truth will come out. My idea, which is more or less what I wanted to say in that interview, was that it was a kind of state crime, not that there was a plot behind it, but Pasolini for fifteen years had been persecuted. Every year he had a trial for a book, for a movie, for corrupting children, every year a trial. The people who killed him, who murdered him, I'm sure, were feeling that they were doing a crusade against the corrupter. In some way, they were induced to kill. It's been one of the most atrocious moments of my life.

Scorsese says he looks at your movies for inspiration.

Among the American directors, he's the one I admire the most. For example, I saw *Casino,* almost three hours long, and there's such a desire to invent cinema while everybody's given up, and he's there with every shot thinking that cinema is still able to be invented. It's not something established. It's a fantastic quality. When I see a movie of his I feel the desire to go and do a movie.

FILMOGRAPHY

Bernardo Bertolucci was born on 16 March 1940, in Parma, Italy.

Paradiso e inferno (1999)
L'Assedio (1998)
Stealing Beauty (1996)
Little Buddha (1993)
The Sheltering Sky (1990)
The Last Emperor (1987)
La Tragedia di un uomo ridicolo (1982)
La Luna (1979)
1900 (1976)
Ultimo tango a Parigi (1973)
Il Conformista (1970)
La Strategia del ragno (1970)
Amore e rabbia (1969)
Partner (1968)
Il Canale (1966)
Via del petrolio (1965)
La Commare secca (1962)
Prima della rivoluzione (1962)

Franco Brusati
Talks About *The Sleazy Uncle*

With a title like *The Sleazy Uncle*, one can't help mustering up images of dirty old men lifting little girls' skirts. It's unfortunate that a better translation for *Lo Zio Indegno* (its original title) couldn't have been created for a film starring two of Italy's greatest living actors, Vittorio Gassman and Giancarlo Giannini.

"Very difficult translating it in English," apologizes director Franco Brusati from his home in Rome. "There is no term in English that's equivalent for *indegno*. The Dirty Old Man isn't the correct translation because *indegno* also means shameful, a man who's deceptive, dirty. It was used by Anatole France in describing Paul Verlaine. The poet was to be admitted in an academy and France hindered his acceptance by saying that he was *un uomo indegno*."

Brusati, one of Italy's most successful and awarded playwrights, has received critical praise on this side of the Atlantic with his films *Bread and Chocolate* (1974) and *To Forget Venice* (1979), which was nominated that year for an Academy Award for Best Foreign Language Film.

The Sleazy Uncle (completed two years ago but only released in 1991) tells the story of a successful man (Giannini) who teams up with his eccentric, middle-aged uncle (Gassman), a successful poet who causes havoc wherever he goes. Brusati, who also wrote the story and the screenplay, is adamant in neither romanticizing the poet for his amoral outrageousness, nor in downgrading the nephew for his conformist lifestyle.

"I wanted to simply paint a portrait of a man who is totally free of conventions," he explains in his native language. "But I did not want to make an apologia. There is a very clear phrase where, after his nephew asks him if all poets are like him, he answers, 'No. Not in the least. There are poets who have a wife and children, they get up at dawn, and maybe even have another job.'

"What I was trying to say was that his God-given talent has nothing to do with his moral qualities. Sometimes they may coincide, sometimes they may not. Just think of Amadeus or Verlaine — the gift that God has given them had nothing to do with their morality on this earth."

Yet the differences in the moral fibre of the characters in the film are so extreme, it's difficult to understand if there's envy between them or disgust.

"Solitaries on one hand are incapable or even ironic in regards to the world of things simple and common," elaborates Brusati. "On the other hand, though, they also envy it. That is, while he despises his nephew for his consumerism, at the same time he slightly envies him.

"He sees him surrounded by his family, the wife, the children — the two envy each other. Like *Tonio Krueger* by Thomas Mann, which talks about envy mixed in with a tip of disgust that intellectuals have for those who are simple. They are two contrasting emotions: while the uncle despises his nephew's mediocrity, he also envies it."

As in most Italian films, all the female characters in *The Sleazy Uncle* are depicted as slightly more than sexual objects. "I disagree," responds Brusati. "The first woman [played by Stefania Sandrelli] yes... but the wife [Andrea Ferreol] is in actuality a very intelligent woman who understands the uncle's poetry better than her husband; and, better than her husband, she understands the danger that occurs when a mediocre man, like her husband, meets an extraordinary man like his uncle.

"Not only is she not a sexual object, but she is, yes, a simple woman, but a much more intelligent and refined person than her husband."

FILMOGRAPHY

Franco Brusati was born in 1922, in Milan, Italy. Died 28 February, 1993, in Rome of leukemia.

The Sleazy Uncle (1989)
Il Buon soldato (1982)
Dimenticare Venezia (1979)
Pane e cioccolata (1973)
Il suo modo di fare (1969)
Il Disordine (1962)

Steve Buscemi
Talks About *Trees Lounge*

Most remember him as the manic Mr. Pink in Quentin Tarantino's *Reservoir Dogs*. Some recognize him as the Buddy Holly waiter in *Pulp Fiction*. Although he's starred in some cool independent flicks *(In The Soup, Parting Glances, Living in Oblivion)* most look at Steve Buscemi as little more than a supporting actor.

Well, they're wrong. Buscemi's presence in films is hardly ever supporting. In the Coen Brothers' *Fargo*, he was instrumental in bridging together the subplots; in Robert Rodriquez's *Desperado* he was the perfect sobering pillar to Antonio Banderas' misery. Now the Brooklyn native tries his hand behind the camera with *Trees Lounge*, a semi-biographical tale about a grown-up slacker who's stuck in a dead-end suburban hometown on Long Island hanging out at the local bar and brooding over his lost girlfriend. A mechanic who can't find a job and who's forced to drive an ice-cream truck for money, Tommy (Buscemi) just can't seem to stay out of trouble.

"That was me," says Buscemi while attending the Toronto International Film Festival. "It's my speculation, had I stayed in Valley Stream, of what would have happened to me. I also based it on other people that I know from there. But, yeah, when I lived in Long

Island that's what I was doing. I worked in a gas station, I drove an ice cream truck and I hung out in bars every night. And before I moved out of Valley Stream I was working in a gas station that was right down the street from me and I was hanging out at a bar that was right across the street from that. So my world got really, really small. If I didn't get out, I don't know what would have happened, because it just wasn't working for me."

So what got him out?

"I was taking acting classes in Manhattan and one of the guys in my class, who was living on Avenue A in the Lower East Side, took a trip and he asked me if I wanted to sublet his apartment," remembers Buscemi. "I did it thinking that I would just do it for the summer and then come back home. The first few weeks were tough. But after about a month of living in Manhattan I just knew that I would never go back to Long Island and that if I was going to be serious about acting that that's where I had to be. And I just decided, then, that it doesn't matter how long it takes, if I want to act this is where I have to be and I have to start doing that."

In watching *Trees Lounge* the viewer notices the intimate interaction between the many characters (the film also stars Anthony LaPaglia, Samuel L. Jackson and Steven Randazzo), whereas the plot is minimal. Buscemi admits that he studied John Cassavetes' movies in order to learn how to develop the relationships.

"His films are character-driven," explains Buscemi. "He doesn't seem to be concerned with the technical aspects of the film, but the performances seem to be really important. And I think there's so many times in films an actor will do the scene and if there's something the slightest bit technically wrong, people just get all upset and worried. And, in his films, it just didn't seem to matter. That's not to say that he didn't have a visual style, because I think his films are really cinematic. But it doesn't matter because you're so caught up in these characters and he never seemed to judge his characters. He just kind of let them do what they do. I just find his work really inspiring."

Like others this year, Buscemi is another actor who decided to try his hand at directing.

"I don't know why I wanted to direct," he says honestly. "Maybe I just wanted more control over my work. I wasn't interested in doing this movie if I couldn't do it the way that I wanted to do it."

FILMOGRAPHY

Steve Buscemi was born on 13 December 1957, in Brooklyn, New York.

ACTOR

Louis et Frank (1998)
Armageddon (1998)
The Wedding Singer (1998)
The Big Lebowski (1998)
The Impostors (1998)
Con Air (1997)
Divine Trash (1997)
The Real Blonde (1997)
Escape from L.A. (1996)
The Search for One-Eye Jimmy (1996)
Kansas City (1996)
Fargo (1996)
Black Kites (1996)
Trees Lounge (1996)

Desperado (1995)
Billy Madison (1995)
Dead Man (1995)
Living in Oblivion (1995)
Things to Do in Denver When You're Dead (1995)
Pulp Fiction (1994)
The Last Outlaw (1994)
Airheads (1994)
The Hudsucker Proxy (1994)
Floundering (1994)
Somebody to Love (1994)
Rising Sun (1993)
Ed and His Dead Mother (1993)
Twenty Bucks (1993)
Reservoir Dogs (1992)
In the Soup (1992)
CrissCross (1992)
What Happened to Pete (1992)
Who Do I Gotta Kill? (1992)
Barton Fink (1991)
Billy Bathgate (1991)
Zandalee (1991)
King of New York (1990)
Force of Circumstance (1990)
Miller's Crossing (1990)
Tales from the Darkside: The Movie (1990)
Slaves of New York (1989)
Mystery Train (1989)
New York Stories (1989)
Bloodhounds of Broadway (1989)
Vibes (1988)
Arena Brains (1988)
Call Me (1988)
Heart of Midnight (1988)
Heart (1987)
Kiss Daddy Goodnight (1987)
Parting Glances (1986)
Coffee and Cigarettes II (1986)
No Picnic (1986)
Sleepwalk (1986)

Director

Trees Lounge (1996)
What Happened to Pete (1992)

Mimmo Calopresti
Talks About *La Seconda Volta*

While the last act of terrorism in Italy occurred nearly fifteen years ago, the implications of the period still echo loudly today. Television news is always reporting on the *pentiti,* those admitting to their guilt in exchange for leniency. But what of the victims of these random acts of horror?

For the first time, a director has brought to the screen a hypothetical situation in which a former terrorist comes face to face with a victim. With *La Seconda Volta* director Mimmo Calopresti has made an intelligent, fascinating and devastating study about the effects Italian terrorism has had on its culprits and victims two decades later. A man (Nanni Moretti) sees the woman (Valeria Bruni Tedeschi) who shot him years earlier out on the street on daily parole. His need to confront her about her motives for shooting him is resisted by her need to forget the incident.

"The idea came after I did some work in a prison with terrorists," explains Calopresti from his home in Rome. "I was able to get to know them and their stories, and once they were able to leave the prison walls during the daytime for work under a new rehabilitation program, I became very curious."

While Calopresti had little trouble doing research on and with former terrorists, he admits to having been greatly embarrassed and awkward when contacting victims of terrorism and their families.

"The closest I got were meetings and conferences held by them," says Calopresti. "I didn't have the courage to meet someone who had undergone such pain. I felt embarrassed to have them tell their story to me directly. Anyway, I was trying very hard to stay away from any sense of 'realism' as far as the characters are concerned. I was afraid to dive too deeply into the 'realistic' side of pain, of suffering. I was embarrassed."

Calopresti is no conventional filmmaker. Whereas an American director could've easily cashed in on the topic by milking the violent angles through flashbacks and stalking, the forty-three-year-old Calopresti preferred to forego all that and concentrate on the main point.

"Which is their meeting," agrees Calopresti. "I purposely avoided the violence, the pain, the mourning. In fact, there is no reconstruction of the fateful incident. I didn't want the violent aspect of the story to deter attention from what the two characters had to say to each other, of that 'meeting.' The most important aspect of the film is the possibility of that meeting. I didn't want any distractions from that."

As for Moretti's involvement — he's also the co-producer — Calopresti credits him for allowing the film to take on non-conventional and artistic freedoms to tell the story.

"If you calculate the last terrorist activities that had occurred in Italy," explains Calopresti, "my characters would have to have been in their fifties, while they're actually in their thirties and forties in the movie. I felt that keeping my characters too imbedded in reality would have made the movie opaque, lifeless. When Moretti decided to accept my invitation to act, he gave me the confidence to free myself from conventional filmic rules and tell the story the way I wanted."

FILMOGRAPHY

Mimmo Calopresti was born in 1955 in Rome, Italy.

La Parola amore esiste (1998)
La Seconda volta (1995)

Michael Corrente
Talks About *American Buffalo*

Who is this Michael Corrente guy who managed to snap away one of the most coveted directing jobs of the decade? For fifteen years Al Pacino had been talking about making a filmic version of David Mamet's wonderful play, *American Buffalo,* as a vehicle, he said, "to expand his astounding performance on Broadway." Then there was James Foley who was overwhelmed by adulation for his version of Mamet's *Glengarry Glen Ross.* Who better to direct this three-hander?

Well, as Mamet wrote in *American Buffalo,* "action talks and bullshit walks."

"That's right," laughs Corrente while attending the Toronto International Film Festival. "There were 200 other people talking about making the movie, while producer Greg Mosher and I wrote out a cheque for the rights and handed it to Mamet. Meanwhile so and so is talking about shooting with three cameras, so and so is talking about his interpretation about how it should be shot, and nobody was paying attention to business which is what the play is about. They were all blowing smoke up each other and finally we put a cheque on the table. So we got the rights."

Not that Corrente is a newcomer. An actor and playwright out Rhode Island, Corrente tried his hand at directing when he adapted his own play *Federal Hill* (about five Italian-American friends) to film. It was *Federal Hill,* in fact that brought him to the attention of Mosher who directed the stage premiere of *American Buffalo* in 1974.

American Buffalo is a biting satire of the American Dream where a compassionate junk store owner, Donny (Dennis Franz) is preparing a heist with his young black protégé (Sean Nelson), but things get messed up when a two-bit hustler, Teach (Dustin Hoffman) brings evil to the scene.

"I think Mamet has a way of taking this incredibly juicy dialogue that we all hear in our lives growing up," says Corrente. "He has a way of taking realistic dialogue and stylizing it so it becomes realistic again on the stage, but with rhythms. It's so juicy and so rhythmic to the ear that it attracts a lot of actors. On the surface it's a movie about three bumbling idiots who couldn't find their ass without a map who think they're going to make the caper of the century and underneath it's about love. I know it sounds goofy but it's about the love that this man has for this kid. Donny, however fucked up as he is, tries to instill some values, some morals in this kid, screwed up as they may be. And they have this relationship in the middle of this shit hole of society that they live in and in comes this tornado that also wants this attention and it's about how we screw each other around in business and then try and justify it."

Corrente, whose family hails from Naples, admits that he saw a side of *American Buffalo* that's rarely portrayed on stage, and that's Donny's story, not Teach's. He also took liberties in casting Bobby's role.

"In the play Bobby has always been cast as a skinny white junkie in his early twenties," explains Corrente. "Dave Mamet went crazy when I told him I was going to cast a black boy. He went nuts. He thought it was brilliant because the more pure he is without being ridiculous the more intense it becomes, the stakes are raised. This is a kid who gets fucked over and he's just a neighbourhood kid with nowhere to go and nobody to look out for him. I've never seen the kid in a play other than a low-life, sniveling, arm-scratching junkie. I grew up with those guys. Those guys are sharper than any fucking junk store owner I've ever seen. They can get a bag of dope more ways than Teach can ever imagine hustling somebody out of a nickel. I thought this kid should be just honest, as pure as you could be without being absurd."

And what does Pacino think about his baby being taken away from under him?

"Pacino had fifteen years to make this movie," smiles Corrente. "When we got the rights we offered the role to him and he didn't get back to us so we assumed he was passing and we moved on to somebody else. I think he passed probably because he couldn't believe that he lost control of it and was not going to have a director forced on him. I think he wanted James Foley to do it. I don't think he liked *Federal Hill* that much and I think he was upset that the rights were just scooped up from underneath him. And rightly so. He should've been upset. Somebody wasn't paying attention and I don't think it was Al."

Filmography

Michael Corrente was born in 1960, in Pawtucket, Rhode Island.

Yellow Handkerchief (2000)
Outside Providence (1999)
American Buffalo (1996)
Federal Hill (1994)

Don Coscarelli
Talks About *Phantasm: Oblivion*

When film student Dan Coscarelli decided to make a sci-fi horror movie about practically nothing, little did he realize that the result would spin out three sequels and a cult following that would endure twenty years. *Phantasm,* with its surreal set pieces and primal scare devices, still stands as one of the most bizarre and original horror movies of all time. Released in 1979, it focuses on thirteen-year-old Michael (Michael Baldwin) who battles gravediggers from outer space, a creepy caretaker dubbed Tall Man (Angus Scrimm), and wonderful silver spheres which attach themselves to people's brains. *Phantasm II* and *Phantasm III* were made years later and now the fourth installment, *Phantasm: Oblivion,* is making its world premiere at Toronto's FantAsia festival.

I talked to Don Coscarelli from his office in Los Angeles.

Why would you continue to make Phantasm *movies for nearly twenty years?*

That's a good question. I would say that obviously the first film was a real passion of mine and subsequent to that the fan response was so tremendous that I decided to do another *Phantasm* and it took a few years to get that off the ground. After that the series became a blessing and curse for me because, on the one hand, I enjoy making the films and I enjoy the feedback, but whenever I'd go out to try and fund any of my other projects it would take awhile and then I'd get an offer to make another *Phantasm*. Rather than be idle I would go ahead and do another *Phantasm* film. We've kinda hit the end of the road with part four because I wanted to answer a few more questions. The movies are notorious for being pretty mysterious so I decided to try to round things up a little more.

Is this the last one?

I think so. You know, we're all getting a little older.

In the first Phantasm *you were also cameraman and editor. That was a lot of work.*

That was a long time ago. I was making an independent movie back before there was an independent film movement. There was so little money that there was no way to pay for a cameraman and an editor. These were the kind of films, being a film student myself, that were being done so it was just a natural outgrowth. The first *Phantasm* was done with a spirit of a student with student-type resources. It turned out well in that respect. The budgets have gotten a little higher and I've been able to get money to hire an editor and a cameraman, but I do miss it a bit.

Where did the idea for Phantasm *come from?*

I had made another independent film prior to *Phantasm* and I had worked with two actors in that film. One was this young boy who became the star of *Phantasm*. I had a long-time desire to work in the sci-fi horror genre and, in this previous film, a family film called *Kenny and Company*, there was one sequence where these kids were in a haunted house on Halloween and this monster jumped out and there was a response from the audience who just jumped up and screamed. What I liked to do was a film that was like that from start to finish, completely. Nothing but shocks and surprises. And I wanted to work with Michael again because he was this fabulous young child actor, so I fabricated this story that he could be featured in. I also started to think of these other actors that I've worked with which included Angus Scrimm, the evil character. The inspiration for the movie came from these actors that were friends of mine that I worked with. I was looking for a vehicle that could be kind of spooky and horrific where I could feature them.

Why do you think that after twenty years the Phantasm *series is still so successful?*

I think there are a number of reasons. I didn't think so while making them, but looking back in hindsight, I understand why they're popular. Certainly you have to start with the two icons of the movies which is the character of Tall Man, played by Angus. He really has a power over audiences; they love to be scared by him. People like to watch him do these evil things. Then there's this other icon which is the chrome spheres, which are the killing devices and audiences like to see them do their tricks. I think it's something so out of the realm of the ordinary, it's a form of violence that just could never happen in real life and people enjoy seeing what kind of tricks they can do next.

You have kids. Do you find it harder to make violent films these days?

I think I've tried to be as responsible as possible. I like to separate *Phantasm* films because they're nothing like slasher films where teenagers are having sex and then they're butchered. They've never been like that. As far as the kids go, I obviously have to censor what my kids see and I do feel disturbed when I hear fans who come up to me say, "I saw the first *Phantasm* when I was five years old," and I think your parents have some problems. Generally, the films that I've made, the horror and the violence has been done in good fun. I've actually employed my kids in this last film.

Your family comes from Italy. Are you a fan of Dario Argento and Mario Bava?

Absolutely. Isn't obvious? *[He laughs.]* While I was making the first *Phantasm*, the original *Suspiria* came out and I just found that to be such a spellbinding movie in the way Argento used some elements. There are images that are still with me today and that I've always tried to use in my films. As far as I'm concerned he's a genius.

Are you having a difficult time being a full-time filmmaker these days?

A little. I've done eight movies, half of which are *Phantasm*. Then I did *Beastmaster* and, in 1990, *Survival Quest*. Obviously, I like to work more but it's hard to get funding. In the horror genre you have a tremendous fan base of sci-fi horror fans, and yet few of the studio executives are familiar with the films because they don't "see" them. There's tremendous prejudice unless it's a big blockbuster like *Scream*.

FILMOGRAPHY

Don Coscarelli was born on 17 February 1954, in Tripoli, Libya.

Phantasm: Oblivion (1998)
Phantasm III: Lord of the Dead (1994)
Survival Quest (1989)
Phantasm II (1988)
The Beastmaster (1982)
Phantasm (1979)
Jim the World's Greatest (1976)
Kenny & Company (1976)

Tom DiCillo
Talks About *Box of Moonlight*

Six years ago Tom DiCillo garnered the attention of moviegoers with his offbeat indie movie *Johnny Suede* starring Brad Pitt as a weirded-out youth. Three years later DiCillo immortalized the nightmarish experience of making *Suede* with the terrific low-budget Festival favourite *Living in Oblivion* where Steve Buscemi plays a stressed-out director dealing with an egocentric star. With his new film, *Box of Moonlight,* DiCillo retains the unique and darkly satirical humour of his first two pics. Here Al Fountain (John Turturro) is a pedantic husband and father who attempts to recapture his youth by visiting a childhood haunt. When he runs into the strange Kid (Sam Rockwell), Al soon finds himself doing things he never thought possible.

John Turturro is wonderful in this movie, he shows soul.

Definitely. I think, in this film, he really got a chance to show himself in a way that I don't think has been seen before. God, I was so pleased to see him work that easily, and yet still be always interesting. You're right, he's got a soul.

He told me that he had a bit of a hard time with this role, because he found it very difficult.

Well, it's interesting. Maybe because the part is based, somewhat, on someone I know very well. In my mind I had an image of what this guy was, the way he could move, the way he could talk. And it surprised me that most people reading the script saw Al so differently. It really bothered me. They thought that Al was like this skinny little twerp, anally repressed, barely able to cross the street, because he's so paranoid. It's funny when I told John: "Let's make this guy a cross between Burt Lancaster and Ward Cleaver" because John is very funny. There were many, many different ways that I tried to get him to get excited. But, ultimately, it came down to John. And he's the one who made it real, and he makes it real in every frame.

Where did Box of Moonlight *come from?*

This one came directly out of a response to *Johnny Suede*. I am the first one to admit that *Johnny Suede* suffers, to some degree, from a pacing problem. I never expected the story to be that lethargic. So I said, I'm going to make a movie that will force you to really deal with action, to deal with physical stuff, and it's going to have to be handled cinematically. I wanted to get out of New York City. I wanted to do a film that has none of those trappings of New York hip bullshit. That was one of the real inspirations.

But the story of this man?

I'm always fascinated with characters who appear to be contained, but really moving toward what they think is a direction. Then, suddenly, they run into something, and get knocked off balance. Kafka was tremendous at this. If you look at this film, every time Turturro's character suddenly settles into what he thinks he is fine, something else happens to him. Also, it helps me wrestle with some things that I'm dealing with. I wake up every morning and go through a mid-life crisis. Certain parts of me just go: "What am I doing? Where am I? What am I up to? How am I going to get through this day?" I like characters who think like that.

What I found interesting, and I liked, was the fact that in the end he didn't change that much.

Thank you for pointing that out. Nothing infuriates me more than a sappy bullshit fucking piece of crap in which the sunlight comes out. It fits into this little plastic container of resolution. That never happens. And, yes, it's a movie. You can do whatever you want. Movies should exaggerate life. It infuriates me when I see films that suggest a character has changed.

I understand you had problems with the initial casting.

I must confess that I was not quite confident in my choice for Al Fountain. The well for that kind of an actor in America is very low. We don't have that many strong, humourous actors, who can be emotional. Brando could do it. Belmondo had that quality. Marcello Mastroianni had it. Even Gerard Depardieu, in his own right, still has it. I was lucky that I discovered that in John Turturro.

Filmography

Tom DiCillo was born in 1954, in New York City, New York.

The Real Blonde (1997)
Box of Moonlight (1996)
Living in Oblivion (1995)
Johnny Suede (1992)

Richard LaGravanese Talks About *Living Out Loud*

Already acclaimed as one of the industry's most respected and prolific screenwriters *(The Fisher King, The Horse Whisperer, The Bridges of Madison County, The Ref)* Brooklyn-born Richard LaGravanese has now astounded critics with his directorial debut, *Living Out Loud*. This is an intricate and humourous tale about a forty-something New York divorcee named Judith (Holly Hunter) who must confront the painful issues of abandonment and insecurity until she meets a kindred soul in elevator operator Pat (Danny DeVito).

It's remarkable how accurate your understanding of women is.

Well, part of the character is based on my sister who went through a difficult divorce and fell into a depression. But that character is a great deal of me, of my own experiences of feeling isolated, feeling disconnected, abandoned. The reason I use a female character is that I feel that I have more possibilities; I can take her more places creatively than I can with a male who rarely gets angry. But to me she's an extension of myself.

You don't think that men get angry too?

No, I think they express it in a different way. I think that men are deeply angry, they just don't know it. They're not as connected emotionally, and they have fewer outlets available to them than women. We've got to face it, we're not that well well-rounded.

Pat's life is as tragic if not more so than Judith's, yet he's more at peace with himself.

Well, there's this saying: a simple-minded man comes home from work thinking about what's for dinner, and an intellectual man comes home from work thinking about all the woes and sorrows he's responsible for and what he has to do to solve them; an enlightened man comes home from work thinking what's for dinner. In Pat it's the simplicity of the man, there is a wisdom that he has more of a heart. Whereas when we first meet Judith, she's more trapped in her mind full thoughts of betrayal and abandonment and self-absorption. As time goes on she gets more and more in her body and in her soul until she reclaims her spirit and finds her way back to who she was. When she says to her husband in the elevator, "I left me long before you did," that's the key idea that she abandoned her own spirit before he ever left her. And him leaving her was really just a manifestation of that.

Did the directing opportunity come first, or did the script?

First was the opportunity to direct, then I wanted to think of something to do. I found these two Chekhov short stories, *The Kiss* and *Misery,* and that's where it started. I combined them with these themes of loneliness and abandonment.

Why?

I'm very intrigued by what's called a Pluto Crisis: your life is like a journey, there is always some underlying interval or pattern or issue that you have to do with, and if you haven't dealt with it by the time you're around forty, it will rise up in the form of a crisis so that you'll look at it almost if as your soul is trying to get your attention. In a way this is the story of a woman's Pluto Crisis, about her self-abandonment and her fighting for a more authentic place in the world, and it would never had happened if her husband had never left her, pulled the rug from under her and woke her up.

You have a sexy lesbian club scene in the film. Where did that come from?

There are two reasons for that. There have been moments in my life where I was actually transformed from experiences in those kind of places where you dance and you reclaim your spirit in your body and not your mind. It's like dancing back into your life. And going back to my sister, there was a time when she was going through a very difficult time in her divorce negotiations, her husband had a great lawyer, and she didn't. So I took her out one night and she saw all this life around her and that's when she made the decision not to battle this petty, meaningless tug-of-war with her husband and to just end it and get on with her life. That idea transpired this sort of transformation.

What's hardest thing about directing?

Stamina. It's a marathon. The mental stamina is a killer and trying to adapt from being a screenwriter which is all about collaborating with a director, to being the person who has the final word, that was a tremendous transition.

Would you do it again?

Oh yes, but right now I'm just concentrating on writing for awhile, and collaborating. I like being alone, which is the other half of writing that I like. Because of the commitment and the energy that I need to direct, I need to find something or write something that I can really connect to.

You studied acting; why not pursue that?

I didn't have the right sensibility for an actor. I did well within my arena, but you can't be an actor if you're embarrassed to rehearse. You have to love being the centre of attention a lot, and I used to hate to rehearse because I used to be embarrassed. I didn't have the right ego. I didn't like the idea about creatively being stalled from doing certain things because of how I looked or my type, things that were out of my control.

Did writing come later?

I started writing short stories when I was nine. But I loved film, and I would connect with the actors but even in acting classes in college I would always write my monologues or plays. The writing was always there but I never paid attention to it.

When did you start paying attention to it?

My wife actually brought it my attention. She's the one that really paid attention to it more than anyone else. I started when I was a part of a comedy act, that's when I met my wife; I was writing a lot of skit comedy and I found that I was fast and that I was good at it, and when I got married, during the first three years, my wife was supporting us and I wrote a play. But she thought that there was little money in theatre and why not write a screenplay? Because of her I wrote *The Fisher King* on spec.

What does sister think of the film?

She thinks it's great. There's a scene in the elevator where she confronts her husband, and that actually happened.

And what do you think your ex-brother-in-law will think?

[He laughs.] Oh my God! He's going to hit the roof!

Filmography

Richard LaGravanese was born in 1957, in Brooklyn, New York.

Living Out Loud (1998)

Anthony Minghella
Talks About *The English Patient*

It takes a mind full of a particularly exquisite imagination to see Venice as the setting for Cairo. Yet those familiar with Anthony Minghella's work weren't surprised to discover that Hôtel des Bains on the Venice Lido actually doubled for Egypt's famous Shepheard's Hotel in *The English Patient*. But Minghella has astounded a good number of people recently for having been able to successfully rewrite Michael Ondaatje's wonderfully cryptic novel into a feature-length movie.

Filmed in Italy and North Africa, *The English Patient* tells the story of a fatally burnt man (Ralph Fiennes) during World War II who finds himself dying in an abandoned monastery in Italy with a French-Canadian nurse (Juliette Binoche) by his bedside. Throughout the three-hour opus we follow the man's memories to his life as an expeditioner in Africa who falls in love with a married British woman (Kristen Scott Thomas).

Director-playwright Christopher Hampton once called Minghella "crazy" for trying to adapt Ondaatje's complicated story into a movie; and few will argue with that statement.

"I hadn't planned on it," laughs Minghella, in town recently to promote the film. "I was saving up Michael's novel while I was finishing a film in New

York. I've read everything he's written before *The English Patient* and was very excited to read his new book. I wasn't intending to pick my way through it as a potential film project, but, after I'd finished reading it, I was so overwhelmed by it. It's such an extraordinary book that I got on the phone to Saul [Zaentz, producer] immediately. Then I collided with my stupidity."

Indeed. Although Minghella — born on the Isle of Wight from Italian parents — had been an award-winning playwright for over a decade *(Made in Bangkok, Love Bites)*, and successfully directed two movies before this *(Truly, Madly, Deeply* and *Mr. Wonderful)*, he'd never tackled anything as "epic" as *The English Patient* before.

"Obviously the most distinguishing characteristic of this novel is that it's so fragmented and mosaic-like," agrees the forty-two-year-old director. "That its gifts, in a way, are very elusive and are very much connected with the beauty of language which is probably the thing that the film is least good in conveying. So obviously I collided them with the realities of what it would mean to make some kind of story structure, some architectural structure which could bring in as many of these beautiful things that I've found in the book as possible, and that wasn't easy."

By watching *Truly, Madly, Deeply* and *Mr. Wonderful*, as well as *The English Patient*, one can easily accuse Minghella of being a hopeless romantic in constant pursuit of the perfect love story.

"Actually, I'm not particularly interested in love," he smiles. "When people talk about the love stories in this film, I'm as intrigued by the love between a nurse and her patient, the love between friends as I am in the sexual love in the film. What seems to me more appealing in this story is that it looks at intimacy, it looks at personal exchanges and says this is not something that is actually private, ultimately, it's about how the world relates to each other as individuals. I tried to describe as accurately as I could what people are as individuals because I'm most interested in the way that people are as members of communities."

One of the biggest problems in transferring a successful novel to film is the amount of material that gets lost in the translation, but Minghella credits the author for having assisted on the script rewrites throughout the arduous shoot.

"I think there are huge casualties in this kind of adaptation," he confesses. "There were things that were in the first draft of the script which we were all very proprietorial of and wanted to see in the finished film. There's this unnecessary ruthlessness that occurs when you can't have another two hours of the film, and so you make thousands of decisions, but we made them collectively. But they were are made in the spirit of trying to appreciate a book that we all loved and at the same time understand the fact that ninety percent of the audience going to see this film wouldn't have heard of *The English Patient*. I hope they run off and buy the book after seeing the film. Our first obligations as filmmakers is to tell a story. The novel's interests are much more opaque and exquisite. And Michael was with us from the first day. One of the things he did, which I think is extraordinary, was rather than look after his book, he looked after the screenplay because at some point I had to stop being the screenwriter of this film and start being the director."

FILMOGRAPHY

Anthony Minghella was born on 6 January 1954, in Ryde, Isle of Wight, U.K.

Cold Mountain (1999)
The Talented Mr. Ripley (1999)
The English Patient (1996)
Mr. Wonderful (1993)
Truly, Madly, Deeply (1992)

Nanni Moretti
Talks About His Career

Italian film director Nanni Moretti gives three reasons he believes his films have never been released in North America.

"First, *i film Europei d'autore,* or art films, are difficult to distribute because they're far removed from the North American culture," he says. "Second, Italy has a problem in marketing its own cultural products. And finally, my films are very personal. I never bother to think wether the Italian public will understand them, never mind worring about what North Americans might think."

There's an unnerving self-confidence in Moretti's tone that borders on arrogance. It's this self-assurance, this determination to do things his way or no way, that has allowed him to create some of Italy's most unique and individualistic movies.

The spotlight at the Festival of Festivals in Toronto for 1993, Moretti makes films that reflect and dissect his country's diverse and, often times, contradictory philosophies. A complete auteur who writes, directs and stars in his own films, Moretti places himself at centre stage and proceeds to tear away at those metaphysical issues he so clearly values. Especially politics.

A devout communist — altough never card-carrying — Moretti is his party's worse critic. In the movie *Palombella Rossa* (1989), arguably his masterpiece, Moretti expresses his anguish at the failure of the communist ideal. Here, he plays a young politician stuck competing in an important water-polo match. During serves, Moretti conducts brilliant monologues on the meaning of communism, occasionally lashing out at journalists, comrades, and admirers hovering around the pool. This is no ordinary film. Free from the constraints of normal film narrative, Moretti's Michele (a recurring character in his films) bounces back and forth between television appearances, discussions with his wife, scenes from *Doctor Zhivago* — another meditation on communism — and violent encounters in the pool.

Brutally intelligent, Moretti makes light of these issues with cutting-edge satire and humour.

"When one makes autobiographical films, irony becomes obligatory," he explains. "When one talks about himself, he should take himself seriously only if he makes fun of himself as well. Otherwise he becomes ridiculous."

"I've always made films on persons and environments where I've always festered a dual relationship of affection and hatred," continues Moretti. "Since I was fifteen years old living in Roma, I've had this intimate relationship with left-wing youth and communism. That's why I feel so critical about it."

Moretti insists that, although his movies are preachy, his goal is to provide the filmgoer with a more cerebral form of entertainment.

"I've always avoided making films that are uselessly anguishing to the viewer," he explains. "When I began making movies I found a formula I felt comfortable with. I made films that were fun and that made one suffer, but not at the expense of the viewer. In the same film I like to alternate comical elements with dramatic ones. This is a way of disorienting and surprising the viewer.

"What did the Italian left-winger expect of *Palombella Rossa?* The usual militant in crisis where the downfall of his personal life coincides with his political career. No. Instead I made a metaphorical picture, one with less realism."

However, when Moretti tackles the more personal issues of love, religion and responsiblity, his character, though still humourous, takes on a disturbing righteousness and anger.

In the quirky *Bianca* (1984), Michele is a mathematics teacher obsessed with his neighbours and colleagues. He meddles in their business and punishes them when they disappoint his view of what the idyllic family should be. In the beautiful *La Messa è finita* (1985) Moretti plays a priest, Don Giulio, assigned to his first parish. Here, he's unable to cope with the seemingly happy lifestyles of his parishioners. He gets angry with the former priest — now married — for loving his son too much, and even scolds the hostess at a dinner party for wearing slippers instead of uncomfortable shoes.

"What Don Giulio and Michele have in common," explains Moretti, "is the desire to become artistic directors in the private lives of others. By living someone else's reality they can escape their own disappointng one. This, naturally, causes the downfall of both of them."

"These characters are not based 100 percent on me," he smiles. "They're born from inside of me, but throughout the film the characters take on their own autonomy. I'll admit that the characters in my films do and say things I would like to do and say in real life. My characters are violent, and I've never hurt anyone in my life, but I often think of getting into physical fights with people. That's why, in my films, I let my characters do those things that I'm suppressed from doing."

Asked if the mini-revolution happening in his country right now is having an affect on his political views, he flashes a skeptical smile. Politicians, he believes, are not the only sinners.

"Right now, maybe for the first time in Italy, exists a political class that's better than the average citizen," sighs Moretti. "Up until this past year it was only a little worse. What's missing in Italy is civic responsibility, the feeling of belonging, and the fault lies mainly with your average person.

Italian citizens are not real citizens, they're not part of a community. The majority of the people have no pleasure in doing their job right, there's no solidarity, but, worst of all, is the lack of respect for laws. And this is just as true for the average man as it is for the politician. In Italy, a person's most coveted quality is cunning, the ability to rip off your fellow man. We have to fight to change all of this, but it'll take many years. I'm not holding my breath."

For Moretti, forty, filmmaking did not come easy. He couldn't study at Rome's famed Centro Sperimentale di Cinematografia because he lacked a university degree (a prerequisite for the Centro), and he was unable to find a director under whom to apprentice (his choices were the Taviani brothers and Marco Bellochio).

Learning the trade as he went along, Moretti produced two Super 8mm shorts *(Pâte da bourgeois,* and *Come parli, frate)*, and directed his first feature *Io sono un autarchico* (1976) for only $3,000. This behind-the-scenes look at an experimental theatre group became a hit at art houses in Rome where it played for five months. Soon after a producer offered Moretti financing to produce another film, *Ecce Bombo.* Following the film's screening at the 1978 Cannes festival, critics worldwide were scrambling for superlatives to praise the young director. Since then Moretti has started his own company, *Sacher Films,* and opened his own art-house cinema in Rome where he screens independent films from around the world.

"I've never had to compromise and I've always stuck to my style," says Moretti. "I've done things alone, and that's how I'd like to stay."

FILMOGRAPHY

Giovanni Moretti was born on 19 August 1953, in Brunico, Bolzano, Italy.

Aprile (1998)
Opening Day of Close-Up (1996)
Caro diario (1994)

La Cosa (1990)
Palombella rossa (1989)
La Messa è finita (1985)
Bianca (1983)
Sogni d'oro (1981)
Ecce Bombo (1978)
Io sono un autarchico (1976)
Come parli, frate? (1974)
La Sconfitta (1973)

Greg Mottola
Talks About *The Daytrippers*

Filmmaking isn't an easy job, and Greg Mottola figured that out the hard way. The Long Island native set off with one project, was forced into another, and the institution that he was convinced supported him wouldn't even consider his work.

"Sometimes you feel like killing yourself," laughs the director.

Well, things aren't that bad. His first movie, *The Daytrippers,* is a funky and quirky comedy about a dysfunctional family that's stuck in a car as they travel into Manhattan to uncover a deception. Produced by Steven Sodebergh *(sex, lies and videotape),* the film received praises at film festivals around the world.

"The film was sold in Italy to Cecchi Gori," says Mottola whose father emigrated from Avellino. "Unsurprisingly the Italians related to the domineering mother. It was the only country where there were different distributors fighting to get the movie at the Cannes Film festival."

A student at the Sundance Writers/Directors Lab, Mottola originally wanted to get his script *Lush Life* produced, and even though actors Campbell Scott and Annabella Sciorra were attached to it, he was forced to go with a less-expensive project.

"I still think the script is good, but it's not an easy sell," says Mottola of *Lush Life*. "And it had a downer ending. People were looking at me as first-time director... I couldn't get the money. I was very frustrated and I was afraid to make a movie really cheaply because I didn't want it to be shoddy. Then Sodebergh asked me if I had something that could be done cheaply, and I realized this was the perfect story. It was such an unromantic view of these people's lives, that it didn't need amazing production values."

Although filmed on a low budget, *The Daytrippers* still features an impressive cast of cameos, including Scott, Stanley Tucci, Parker Posey and Hope Davis.

"I was afraid to ask Campbell to be in this," admits Mottola. "Then I realized that these actors really feel like they're rarely allowed the opportunity to sink their teeth into a part, and really collaborate with a director when they work. It was surprisingly easy, once they read the script, to convince them to do it."

The Daytrippers, Mottola explains, is inspired by his own family: an image of him crammed with the rest of the clan in the back of the car while discussions run rampant.

"What's crazy is, that even now as an adult, when I travel in the car with my parents, it's like nothing's changed," he says. "I was just sitting there, in the back of the car recently feeling like I was a kid again, a child, and my parents are treating me that way. The story itself, though, came out of this desire to tell a funny story about the inherent contradictions in these kind of relationships, how you basically need your family.

It's pure quirk of fate that you're attached to them for your entire life."

What came as a surprise to Mottola was the film's rejection at the Sundance Film Festival, even though his script for *Lush Life* was developed there.

"I was disappointed with their response to the film," says Mottola. "I felt like they didn't really get the movie, and I was a little surprised. I think they missed the point of the movie."

Instead, Mottola submitted the film to rebel film festival, Slamdance, created by a bunch of filmmakers who didn't make it into Sundance in the past and located just several miles away from Sundance.

"I thought it was a cool idea," says Mottola. "The thing that sucked about it is they had no money and the Sundance people were very hostile toward them. In the first screening the sound system was horrific and the projectors were in the same room and there was one speaker in the front and it was wired badly. It sounded so bad, they had to turn it up really loud, so you could maybe understand the dialogue and the people in the back could hear it over the sound of the projectors, but the people in the front all had their fingers in their ears. It was so loud and distorted and horrific. It was the first screening of the film ever and it was the worst possible conditions. I was ready to kill myself. But our second screening went much, much better. It was getting our foot in the door."

But Mottola isn't giving up on *Lush Life*. Following the critical success of *The Daytrippers,* there's a good chance that funding for his second flick isn't too far behind.

Filmography

Greg Mottola was born in 1960, in the Bronx, New York.

Actor

Independent's Day (1998)
Celebrity (1998)
Loser (1991)

Director

The Daytrippers (1996)
Swingin' in the Painter's Room (1989)

Maurizio Nichetti
Talks About *Luna e l'altra*

Although Maurizio Nichetti was already well-respected in his native Italy for his brilliant comedic turns, his unique talents weren't appreciated on this side of the Atlantic until the release of his third film, *The Icicle Thief,* in 1988.

A disarming comedy, that's often very funny, the movie was an amusing satire on the ruin of cinema by television. His following film, *Volere volare* (1990), was every bit as inventive, charming and audacious as he stretched out in new ways by employing animation techniques to explain a man's metamorphoses in the face of temptation.

In his newest film, *Luna e l'altra,* Nichetti once again tackles the concept of displaced personalities in his signature gentle and loving manner.

Set in 1955, the movie tells the story of an elementary school teacher, *Luna* (Iaia Forte) who's transferred from Naples to Milan to teach a group of rambunctious children. The woman, who lives alone with her father, is unaware that the school's janitor (played by Nichetti) is in love with her but sees her life drastically changing when, following the theft of a magic lantern, she loses her shadow which begins to take on a personality of its own.

"I usually make comedies that deal with real and social situations," explains Nichetti from his home in Italy. "But always with a fantastical twist to them. My films are always very real, very realistic, and they always deal with emotional or social situations. *The Icicle Thief* dealt with problems between film and television, while *Volere volare* was a love story told in a very bizarre manner. I guess you can say that there's a love story here hidden within the movie that somewhat has a happy ending. While in *Volere volare* the happy ending came via the man's transformation into a cartoon character, here it happens through the protagonist's personality split."

Nichetti admits that the shadow idea is borrowed from the Peter Pan tale, while the personality split has always been a favourite plot device used in comedies.

"For me it was an interesting and original way to tell a story that's set in the 1950s when society wasn't yet conditioned by television," he explains. "In Italy, in those days, politics were very simple with boundaries that were very well-defined and clear. Today things are much more complicated. The movie reflects all of this. For example *Luna*, who's an elementary school teacher. In those days the atmosphere in primary schools was very disciplined, almost nostalgic. Her adventure with the shadow is a form of rebellion against that scholastic order, a desire to escape a reality that was too nostalgic of an Italy of years past. Although the film is not political, the political climate of the country in the 1950s is well represented."

There's little question that Nichetti is a talent of deep intelligence who lets serious matters subtly seep through his pictures, but never for long. A lover of comedy and its influence on the human condition, Nichetti believes that laughter is the only alternative to an increasingly dismal reality.

"I'll always make comedies," he says. "I think that in life there are already too many excuses not to be happy. In everyday life, in the papers, on television, we hear about anguish, anxiety, fear and war. I believe that cinema should reflect serious matters but always in a manner that's much more relaxed than reality. That's why I'm always struggling, with comedy, to confront existential problems but with a smile."

FILMOGRAPHY

Maurizio Nichetti was born on 8 May 1948, in Italy.
Luna e l'altra (1996)
Palla di neve (1995)
Stefano Quantestorie (1993)
Volere volare (1991)
Ladri di saponette (1989)
Il Bi e il Ba (1985)
Domani si balla! (1983)
Ho fatto splash! (1982)
Ratataplan (1979)

Al Pacino
Talks About *Looking for Richard*

For most of his career, Al Pacino has battled with restless commitment coming to grips with Shakespeare. In his directorial debut, *Looking for Richard*, the actor was determined to demystify the Bard's fabled texts by combining documentary, performance and interviews with subversive students while attempting to stage *Richard III*. Starring Alec Baldwin, Winona Ryder, Aidan Quinn and Kevin Spacey, as well as appearances by Vanessa Redgrave, Kenneth Branagh and Sir John Gielguld, *Looking for Richard* is proof that Shakespeare's work is timeless... even in 1996 Manhattan.

Why Richard III *rather than* Hamlet *or* Macbeth *or any of the others?*

Richard was the play I was most familiar with. I think that it's a more complicated play, *Richard*, because it's a history play and when it's taken out of context from the *Henrys, War of Roses*, it's difficult to understand. So had I done another play as much, I would have done it, but *Richard* was the most familiar to me.

While you were doing Richard *were you subconsciously looking for Pacino?*

Yes. Because it's a question of always doing that, I think; it's always looking for yourself in some way in the character you're playing or whatever you're doing. At least that's what I find, because you find out a lot about yourself in those situations.

Your Richard isn't very stagy. Would you have done it differently with another director?

I probably would have done a *Richard* differently. Part of my *Richard* in this film is part-Richard and part an illustration of *Richard*. So sometimes I would do the limp and sometimes I was trying to get across another thing. For instance, in the Lady Ann sequence, if you notice I have a look of a more romantic hero-type while I'm doing it, only as a kind of way of projecting that aspect of the encounter between the two of them. That's why sometimes there's a limp and sometimes there isn't. And sometimes we're doing it in costume and sometimes we're not — but that's all part of the style of the picture.

As an American, do you have an intimidation with Shakespeare?

You're not as encouraged, in America, to do the Shakespeare plays, simply by the very nature of what's available to us. A certain kind of presentation is expected, because the great English actors who have come across to show us what they have done with it, is so special, and so lauded by us in America, so the tendency is to feel that it's something that belongs in another part of the world. However, we have our own interpretations of it and we do it in the theatres throughout the country and have come to learn about it. I personally learned of it through the films of Olivier and some of the American films from Orson Welles to *Julius Caesar* with Marlon Brando early on in my life.

So my connection came through the movies. And then, of course, later on when I went to see the Shakespeare movies, like Zeffirelli's *Romeo and Juliet,* which I think was a great thing. I think we had a major breakthrough here with Kenneth Branagh and *Henry V.* I think he opened the gates for Shakespeare.

You talk about opening up Shakespeare in terms of American acting. Is humour an integral part of that?

Yeah. We really tried to get the humour. I think there's a kind of innate humour and irony in this play. You find it in all of the Shakespeare plays, even the tragedies. I think that part of what makes the more dramatic and the tragic elements of these plays more palatable is if you balance it with humour. It sheds a light on it sometimes or makes it more tolerable for an audience when some of those things happen to have humour there.

It must have been distressing to hear the kids in the park say, "Shakespeare is just boring." Is this in an indictment to the American school system?

I wouldn't think so. I think it's a question of that's how some people feel. I think it's also how we're exposed to it, how we're brought into it. I know I had my own long, drawn-out story about how it happened to me, which I don't want to take your time up with now.

Take my time.

It has something to do with the earlier teachers I had. I was just lucky enough to have a woman, a Blanche Rothstein, who taught me in junior high school and who involved me in Shakespeare in a way that made it personal and made me enjoy it. But I was lucky. And sometimes that will happen. In part, it starts in the home, in the schools, like everything else.

Did you think of bringing this to the universities?

Yeah. The whole spirit of this movie is a kind of experiment, that's how it started. It took on this kind of life. I thought that if I kept moving along with it, that it might make its way into the archives. But if it went further, it was going to go to schools. And then we thought possibly, down the line, it would be a television sort of mini-thing over a four- or five-night period with interviews and people talking about it. Then it became a movie. That's something that only happened about a year ago. I've been doing this thing almost three-and-a-half or four years now. The initial impetus came out of a desire to communicate it to schools.

You played Richard *on stage some fifteen or twenty years ago. Then this. Are you going to put* Richard *to rest, or pick him up again in ten years?*

Anything like that could happen. That's usually the way it is with the classic pieces. It happens, because when you talk to Kenneth Branagh he will tell that he will do his *Hamlet* for the third or fourth time. So there's a kind of a revisiting of the great roles. I think it's traditional with actors, so it's possible I could *Richard* again. I don't know whether it's probable, but it is possible. I would like to do another Shakespeare, more like something like *Titus Andronicus*.

What was your interpretation of the role over fifteen years?

The first time when I first did it when I was younger, I was able to do contortions with my body and move around in a way that I don't know — I was in my twenties. I tried it in my thirties, I couldn't do it. So I wound up doing it more like a spider. And then now I sort of just try to do it in a chair as much as possible.

Are you going to do more directing?

The directing aspect of this movie was a natural extension of myself. It seemed natural that I would make a film about it. I knew someone else was going to direct it. But I had this concept. And when the other person had another commitment I thought that it would be easier if I stayed and did the concept myself. I enjoy the whole thing of making pictures, because when you make pictures as an actor, your relationship to film is one way. When you make it as a director, your relationship is another. And the thing I have found in making the movie is your relationship is a much more tactile one, a more personal one, it's a more inclusive one and it's a lot of fun. You have a lot of control. There are directors who can make great films and also make good films, because they're so talented and they have such craft and they spend a lifetime doing it. I spent a lifetime acting, so my perception, the way I look at things, is coming through that whole idea of acting.

You put your own money into the show.

Yes. When I'm going to experiment or try something, I'd rather take it from what I've got and do it all that way. If it includes the financial, then it's the financial, too. I think that it affords you a freedom. A lot of what we do is dictated by the clock. And how I mean that is we even form techniques and ways of looking at things, because the clock is dictating. When you're taking care of the finances yourself, sometimes it's not necessary to do that. Now, me, for example, I would still be cutting *Richard* and shooting *Richard,* so when it comes to that I can't be stopped but I do feel restrictions are good up to a point, because sometimes they do work.

Why did you originally become an actor and did your grandfather have some influence?

Yeah. He wanted me to be a baseball player, so that's what I wanted to be, too. But he did have an influence on me. But my mother also was the most encouraging about acting, because she was much more literate and much more interested in those kinds of things. She was my biggest encourager, my mother.

Why did you want to act?

It seemed like a good idea at the time. I enjoyed the animation of it. I enjoyed what it was. I wasn't sure I wanted to do it, so I just went through school and a lot of times, I tell you, it beat going to class because I got in to the shows there, so it was easier. And I got passed subjects, passed in everything, because I was in the shows.

Filmography

Alfredo James Pacino was born on 25 April 1940, in New York City, New York.

Actor

Chinese Coffee (1999)
The League (1999)
Man of the People (1999)
The Devil's Advocate (1997)

Donnie Brasco (1997)
Looking for Richard (1996)
City Hall (1996)
Heat (1995)
Two Bits (1995)
Jonas in the Desert (1994)
Carlito's Way (1993)
Glengarry Glen Ross (1992)
The Godfather Trilogy: 1901-1980 (1992)
Scent of a Woman (1992)
Frankie and Johnny (1991)
The Godfather Family: A Look Inside (1991)
The Godfather: Part III (1990)
Dick Tracy (1990)
Sea of Love (1989)
The Local Stigmatic (1989)
Revolution (1985)
Scarface (1983)
Author! Author! (1982)
Cruising (1980)
...And Justice for All (1979)
Bobby Deerfield (1977)
Dog Day Afternoon (1975)
The Godfather: Part II (1974)
Scarecrow (1973)
Serpico (1973)
The Godfather (1972)
The Panic in Needle Park (1971)
Me, Natalie (1969)

DIRECTOR

Chinese Coffee (1999)
Looking for Richard (1996)

Leone Pompucci
Talks About *Mille Bolle Blue*

Those familiar with Mina's famous 1961 hit *Mille Bolle Blu* can attest to the ditty's infectious and repetitive title line. Bubbly and tricky in its tongue-twisting way, children of the time sang it continually while the adults danced to it seductively.

In his first feature film of the same name, director Leone Pompucci resorts back to his childhood memories of the time detailing two days in the lives of the inhabitants of a middle-class apartment block in Rome on the eve of the famous eclipse.

While the children play on the building's rooftop, a Neapolitan escapee visits his wife; in another apartment Mr. Rossi just died and his vulturous children can't wait to rip each other off of the inheritance. Beautiful Elvira, meanwhile, is preparing for her upcoming marriage while her lovelorn ex-boyfriend, Antonio, pines for her in the nearby bar. Then there's Guido, blind since birth, who has to wait a few more days before discovering if the eye operation he underwent will restore his sight.

"These are all real characters of my childhood," says Pompucci from Rome. "As you noticed, they all have different Italian accents and mannerism. Rome, after the war, was the place where everyone came to live, particularly from the south. One day I read in the newspaper about an escapee who died after he slipped from the roof during an uprising, and they printed his photo. This sparked memories of my childhood and my neighbourhood and the apartment block where I grew up. It's the world that weighed on my childhood."

A world, he admits, that has changed maybe too much.

"There's probably less ingenuity, or at least a different kind," he says. "*Mille Bolle Blu* is a film about ingenuity but of a geographical ingenuity, the courtyards before there was light, open spaces where children could run freely screaming their heads off. Today there are less children and less sounds of that kind. We're still a bit ingenuous, but not as much as we need to be to survive happily."

Pompucci explains that he set *Mille Bolle Blu* — a winner at the Venice, Switzerland and Stockholm film festivals, as well as the coveted Donatello — in 1961, the year of his own birth, because he remembers the wild stories his mother had told him about Italy's only eclipse in one hundred years.

"She would tell me about the chickens who laid bizarre eggs and cows that gave birth to strange calves," he explains. "So I thought it would be nice to set this magical phenomenon in my movie, as a gift from God or the stars to these characters. For thirty seconds or a minute, like a time-out, everyone can stop and think in the darkness about their lives and are given the opportunity to change events, but when the light comes back, they don't, they go along the same direction. Truthfully, the dark moment gives an opportunity for enlightenment, but when the sun returns, they're as blind as before.:

A unique and compassionate gaze at the past, *Mille Bolle Blu* also features the filmmaker's gorgeous photographic style.

"More than a filmmaker, I'm a painter," confesses Pompucci. "So I incorporated all those visual techniques of my work into this film. You see, I want events in the movie to be simultaneous. I believe we all do things for ourselves that we believe are important for us, and I wanted to convey that with my camera."

FILMOGRAPHY

Leone Pompucci, was born in 1961, in Rome, Italy.

La Pecora e il lupo (1997)
Camerieri (1995)
Mille bolle blu (1993)

Gabriele Salvatores
Talks About *Mediterraneo*

When Italian actors Diego Abatantuono and Claudio Bigagli landed on a remote Greek island in the Dodecanese region of the Aegean sea — not unlike the characters they were to portray in the movie *Mediterraneo* — they were certain that their director, Gabriele Salvatores, had gone off his rocker.

Not much larger than a rock, the island had a sole hotel with only two rooms available... and not a restaurant in sight! With a cast and crew of forty-five, and a scorching summer heat of 40 to 45 degrees Celsius, what was Salvatores thinking?

"Anguish," he says with a smile. "I wanted the actors to experience the anguish of being stuck on a faraway island... just like their characters."

He wasn't kidding. Portraying Italian soldiers abandoned on a remote Greek island during World War II after being sent to occupy it, the actors had to wear the same flannel clothing that actual soldiers wore during the war, and were forced to live with local fishermen whose conditions hadn't improved since the 1940s.

After two months of filming, cast and crew were eager to get home... even if it meant paddling across the Aegean.

"I have this habit of filming in sequence," explains the director, sitting comfortably in his Toronto hotel suite. "Just like their characters. I wanted the actors to slowly get used to the heat, the food, the sea... I wanted them to relax and slowly shed their clothing. And that's exactly what happened."

The result is Italy's largest box-office grossing Italian film in the past ten years. Since *Mediterraneo*'s release in Italy, the film has brought in roughly $50 million, a staggering amount considering that in the past twenty years American films were the only ones filling Italian movie theatres.

Salvatores believes that timing — the film was released at the beginning of the Gulf War — was a major factor in its popularity.

"At the time, in Italy, there was a lot of talk about desertion," he says. "Either non-intervention on the part of the state, or, if you were drafted, outright refuse. The film, because of its underlying anit-war message, became a symbol of this protest in Italy."

Based on a book titled *L'Armata Sagap (I Love You Army)*, written by a sergeant of an Italian regiment whose group of soldiers quit playing war and formed a communal family on a Greek island, *Mediterraneo* is the third in a series of films by Salvatores, forty-one, that deal with his generation's attitudes toward growing up.

Marrakech Express (1988) tackled the desire to remain children, to remain in a group with friends, and the fear of finding oneself alone in the world. The second film, *Turné* (1989), dealt with two characters who represented different aspects of Salvatores' generation: a radical, idealistic character and a more staid, consumerist one.

In *Mediterraneo*, Salvatores wanted to approach what he believes is a fundamental problem of his generation in Italy: that of escaping from a society that's continually changing.

"My generation has taken flight many times," he says. "In the 1960s and 1970s it was with political commitment and drugs. Then in the 1980s we fled from politics with consumerism. I wanted to somehow portray this personal desire to escape, but I needed a metaphor."

Which he found in World War II, after reading the true story of Italian soldiers who, distanced from the war and from society on a remote Greek island, slowly stopped being soldiers and integrated with the local islanders.

"It's important to add that Greece, for my generation in Italy, signifies the fist trip away from home, the 'first flight.' For many Italian eighteen-year olds, Greece is were you first go on vacation alone."

A law student in Milan during the politically turbulent 1960s, Neapolitan-born Salvatores decided to quit his studies ("My father, who's an attorney, didn't speak to me for two days") to join the theatre as a means of expressing political thought... what he calls "propaganda theatre."

In 1972, he formed what is today Italy's most prestigious and important theatre company, Teatro Elfo, but confesses that his first love has always been film. "In the early 1970s, in Italy, it was nearly impossible to make movies. The only films were horrible Hollywood-influence B-flicks."

Following what he calls nearly fifteen years of "Italian cinema darkness" where the Italian film production industry was practically extinct, there arose a new wave of young Italian filmmakers. Included with Salvatores in the group is Giuseppe Tornatore *(Cinema Paradiso)*, Daniele Lucchetti *(Il Portaborse)*, Marco Risi *(Ragazzi fuori)* and Maurizio Nichetti *(The Icicle Thief)*.

Salvatores — who has never been married — refers to his transition from theatre to film as another changing season in his life... like love. "Theatre is like a marriage," he explains. "You have to keep rekindling the passion through long relationships. Cinema, on the other hand, is passion: brief, condensed. You gamble it all in a shorter period of time.

"And in this particular moment in my life," he smiles coyly, "I'm less disposed towards marriage."

Filmography

Gabriele Salvatores was born on 20 July 1950, in Naples, Italy.

Calcutta Chromosome (1999)
Nirvana (1997)
Sud (1993)
Puerto Escondido (1992)
Mediterraneo (1991)
Strada Blues (1990)
Turné (1990)
Marrakech Epress (1989)
Kamikazen ultima notte a Milano (1987)
Sogno di una notte di mezza estate (1983)

Michele Soavi Talks About *Dellamorte Dellamore*

If there is a thing called Italian Baroque film noir, *Dellamorte Dellamore (Cemetery Man)* is it. A combination of poetry and gore, bizarro and romanticism, the fourth feature by Italian director Michele Soavi is one demented and wild flick.

Based on the comic book, *Dylan Dog*, by Tiziano Sclavi, this ghoulish film tells the story of Francesco Dellamorte (Rupert Everett), a caretaker of the Buffalora cemetery somewhere in Italy. His only companion is a troll-like mute who never leaves him alone. Francesco's job is to smash the skulls of the dead who are coming to life due to some weird epidemic, but after he meets the woman of his dreams (Anna Falchi) — who comes alive after various incarnations — he's not sure he likes his job anymore.

"Lately, in Italy, comic books are enjoying great success," says Soavi, thirty-seven, who was in Toronto recently to promote the movie. "Especially among young boys. *Dylan Dog* was hugely successful because it was able to fuse fear with black humour, and like you well know, Italy isn't known for its black humour."

One of the reasons for the appeal is that Sclavi was also able to spin tales that very much reflected Italy's youth culture by making reference to modern movies, music, literature and art, initiating an unprecedented comic-book craze.

"Following the success of *Dylan Dog,* Sclavi tried to release the book, *Dellamorte Dellamore,*" explains Soavi. "Practically number zero in the story sequence that explains Francesco's origins. But the publishers were too squeamish about the idea of making a hero out of a cemetery keeper. Sclavi had to change some of the characters and settings. The result was the film I wanted to make."

Soavi is no novice to the horror genre. After a brief acting career, he became assistant director to Italy's greatest terror master, *Dario Argento,* working on *Tenebrae, Creepers,* and *Opera.* It was Argento, in fact, who produced his previous films *Deliria, The Church* and *The Sect.*

"I wanted to make a film that surpassed the typical horror genre," admits Soavi. "My previous films could be categorized as 'horror,' but while the visuals may have been interesting, the storylines were pretty banal. *Dellamorte* represents a major step forward for me, not just for the mix of comedy and black humour, but because it deals with important contemporary issues. I believe it reflects the nature of today's teenagers, their loneliness, their desire to not grow up. In fact, the protagonist is thirty years old but he thinks like a thirteen year-old. I tried very hard to explain this parallel between his world, that closed within the cemetary walls that's full of life, green, and animals, and the outside world which is supposed to be of living but is instead is full of boredom. The parallel, in fact, is between the dead living and the living dead: the dead living are more alive than the living dead."

Soavi insists, however, that no comparison whatsoever should be made with George Romero's classics *Night of the Living Dead* and *Dawn of the Dead*.

"*Dellamorte Dellamore* is the story of two unfortunates," he says. "We don't talk about the epidemic that causes the dead to come alive or anything else because the important thing here are these two people, their love for one another."

Although *Dellamorte* is an Italian movie filmed in Italy with mostly Italian stars, Soavi chose to make the movie in English, like his previous films.

"For several reasons," he explains. "My films are much more popular in the U.S. and England than they are in Italy, and I hate the idea of having to dubbed voiceovers. I also like using English actors, and I refuse to have their voices dubbed."

For Soavi, casting Everett *(Comfort of Strangers, Ready-to-Wear)* in the lead was the only choice. "The character is designed after Rupert," laughs Soavi. "Sclavi made Francesco in his image, literally. And Everett just loved the idea of bringing this guy to life. He jumped on the chance."

Filmography

Michele Soavi was born on 3 July 1957, in Rome, Italy.

Dellamorte Dellamore (1994)
La Setta (1990)
La Chiesa (1988)
Aquarius (1987)
Dario Argento's World of Horror (1985)

Giuseppe Tornatore
Talks About *Everybody's Fine*

Six years ago, downtrodden and depressed, twenty-eight-year-old Italian director Giuseppe Tornatore was sitting in the neighbourhood restaurant where he had dinner alone every night.

At the time, his film *Cinema Paradiso* was one of the biggest flops in Italian film history. He was living in a small room in a Rome suburb and was so poor he had struck a deal with the restaurant's owner that he'd pay him a certain sum a month so he could eat there daily.

One evening, in a corner of the restaurant, another customer was having dinner also on his own. He was an older man, very proud-looking and dignified, and next to his chair was a suitcase and a basket held tightly together by rope.

Curious, the young director asked the waiter if he knew the man. He was "someone who travels" *("Uno che viaggia")*, the waiter said.

Tornatore was struck by this phrase. It ate away at him. *Uno che viaggia.* This man was not someone who was going somewhere, but "someone who travels." *Uno che viaggia.*

For months he asked himself: "Where could a man like this be going?" With time the answers came and, slowly, so did the script to his latest film *Everybody's Fine.*

It's the story of Italy as seen through the eyes of the elderly Matteo Scuro (played by Marcello Mastroianni). *Everybody's Fine* follows the retired civil servant as he pays a surprise visit to his five grown children who are now scattered throughout the country.

From Trapani to Naples, Rome, Florence, Rimini, Bologna, Milan and Turin, Matteo discovers a troubled and insane Italy; and when he finally meets with his children, he is confronted with tragic and unsettling news.

Tornatore remembers the spark that prompted him to make the film.

"It was the period immediately following the release of *Cinema Paradiso* in Italy," he says. "When *Cinema Paradiso* was released in Italy, it was one of the biggest disasters in the history of Italian cinema. It didn't make a lira, and no one went to see it. Theatres refused to screen it, and it was eventually taken apart and forgotten."

"For about six months I tried to figure out why. The experience was so discouraging, that for days on end I stayed at home and racked my brain on what went wrong. I was also very broke, and my friends would tell me to make a career change.

"Even though I was in a very bad way, every time someone called and asked how I was, I'd say *bene* (fine), even it wasn't true. I wondered why I kept saying I was fine when I wasn't, so I started asking everyone I met and talked to how they were.

"And everyone always answered that they were fine. I thought, if they're all fine like I'm fine, imagine how they really feel?

"Basically, I found this concept of the inhibition, of the impossibility to say how we really feel in an era where means of mass communication are at their peak... this contradiction that one communicates better long distance than close by, interesting.

"I pieced together the idea of the old man who travels with someone who has to find his children to see how they really are. So I threw all my preoccupations and worries in the garbage, and I started writing the script."

Tornatore was adamant in pointing out that *Everybody's Fine* did not rise from the success of his Oscar-winning *Cinema Paradiso*. "I finished writing the script before *Cinema Paradiso* went to Cannes and gained success," he said.

Whereas *Cinema Paradiso* paid loving tribute to the movies by exposing its mysteries through the fascinated eyes of a young boy and his mentor, *Everybody's Fine* exposes the reality of a country which has seen its many dreams shattered. Its characters are disillusioned and disenchanted, at times almost odious.

"They are surely not *simpatici*," says Tornatore. "But they are not odious. They are only the representatives of the most crowded class of people: those who, in one way or another, never make the news, never make history, never cause gossip.

"They are the souls of purgatory. But most importantly, in order to avoid destroying a man's [Scuro's] dreams, they are people who choose to hide their anguish and their pain. I have a great respect for this type of person."

Born in the now-violent region of Bagheria, Sicily (*Cinema Paradiso* was filmed in his hometown), Tornatore joined Italy's government broadcasting titan RAI Television in the late 1970s, following the success of his first short film, *Il Caretto*.

In 1982, his documentary *Ethnic Minorities in Sicily* won him a prize at the Salerno Film Festival and helped pave the way for his first feature film, *Il Camorrista*, about Neapolitan organized crime.

But it was with his second film, *Cinema Paradiso*, that he was credited with bringing Italian cinema back to international markets. No thanks to his compatriots.

"When cinema in Italy was at its peak fifteen to twenty years ago," he says bitterly, "no one worried about opening a film school; no one worried about making new laws regarding filmmaking. No one ever worried that one day Italian film would need to be protected in Italy.

"After all, things were going great, it wasn't necessary. When things started going not so great, with the recession and all, audiences weren't filling up theatres anymore. So theatres were becoming scarce and those left were catering to foreign product, especially American.

"The 1980s found the country with no new directors. Without film schools, there were no film students, and if a film was released, there were no theatres to screen them."

Hopefully, with young filmmakers like Tornatore, Silvio Soldini and Gianni Amelio, the 1990s may see a resurgence of Italian cinema reminiscent of the golden days of Visconti, Antonioni and De Sica.

FILMOGRAPHY

Giuseppe Tornatore was born in 1956, in Bagheria, Sicily, Italy.

La Leggenda del pianista sull'oceano (1998)
L'Uomo delle stelle (1995)
Una pura formalità (1994)
La Domenica specialmente (1991)
Stanno tutti bene (1990)
Nuovo cinema Paradiso (1988)
Il Camorrista (1985)

Stanley Tucci
Talks About *Big Night*

For us Italians, the fact that eating a good meal can bring us close to nirvana is no big secret. Yet watching food being prepared with love and creativity, and eaten with desire and appreciation, has always been a successful ploy in movies even for those of us brought up on the very best. First there was *Babette's Feast*, then *Tampopo*, then *Eat Man, Drink Woman*. Now, celebrating the very best in Italian cuisine and passion, comes Stanley Tucci's terrific first feature, *Big Night*.

Known for his work as a television *(Murder One)* and movie *(Kiss of Death, The Pelican Brief)* actor, Tucci decided to call on his experiences as an Italian-American to tell the story of how, through the delicious metaphor of food, the American Dream can clash with artistic vision.

It's the 1950s and Primo (*Wings'* Tony Shalhoub) is a master chef who emigrated with his younger brother Secondo (Tucci) to a city on the New Jersey shore to open an Italian restaurant. Problem is that Primo's "obscure" dishes don't sell, and Secondo is so desperate to save the business from bankruptcy, that he holds a lavish dinner with select friends in the hopes that the famous Italian-American singer, Louis Prima, will show and give them the publicity the eatery is so desperately needs to remain in business.

"I wanted to make a movie about artists and the struggle between commerce and art," explains Tucci. "Also, I wanted to show a different view of Italian-Americans. I didn't set out to do those things, but it evolved into those things, but also cinematically there were certain things that I wanted to try, to see if they would work."

Although Tucci's grandparents immigrated from Calabria decades ago the old traditions remain a big part of his family, the Westchester County native insists. But, he adds, no one in his family has ever owned a restaurant.

"The autobiographical side in the movie is only the way people relate to one another but not the relationships exactly," he explains. "Meaning the taciturn quality of both brothers with each other when it comes to saying how they feel and their various explosions that they have, who they take their anger out on, how they deal with each other towards the end of the picture, that's real. It's the opposite of what we usually see as far as Italians are portrayed. They never touch each other in the whole movie until the end. Usually you see much more physicality in films. That's not really my experience growing up."

As for the food — WARNING!— do not see this movie on an empty stomach. For the "big night" the menu consists of — apart from the antipasti and zuppa — a tri-colour risotto (spinach, seafood, quattroformaggi), a timpano, baked salmon, capon stuffed with pomegranates, half roasted pig and a slew of roasted, grilled and sautéed vegetables.

"Meals were so important in my family, and it was a way to express love, to show you care, and it was a way to communicate," remembers Tucci. "Also the art of making food is a beautiful one, and not only making food but creating a dinner party, a pretty difficult but fun thing to do. My parents always did that. I loved it when they did it, the house would change, the whole environment would change, colours, the tables. I loved it."

Even more important than the food presented (if that's possible!), what makes *Big Night* stand out as a forerunner in Italian-American flicks is the way the people are portrayed.

"That's why I set it in the 1950s," says Tucci. "In the 1950s America was really feeling its oats and everybody wanted to achieve the American Dream and America was the be all and end all of everything. Immigrants would come to the country and, if they were marketed as a restaurant or as a shop owner in movies, it was always the extreme version of their cultural identity that was put forth, like spaghetti and meatballs with Italians, and then gangsters. That seemed the reality for Italians in many generations, where the Italian was the gangster, and the restaurant owner served spaghetti and meatballs on red and white checkered tablecloths. What we really wanted to do was take these two guys who made everything by hand and who are very sophisticated and for the most part cultured guys who have an elegance and a delicacy to them and set them against the broad strokes in North America that were prevalent at the time."

Filmography

Stanley Tucci was born on 11 January 1960, in Katonah, New York.

Actor

Joe Gould's Secret (1999)
A Midsummer Night's Dream (1999)
The Impostors (1998)
Winchell (1998)
A Life Less Ordinary (1997)
Deconstructing Harry (1997)
The Eighteenth Angel (1997)
Life During Wartime (1997)
Montana (1997)
Big Night (1996)
The Daytrippers (1995)
Kiss of Death (1995)
Jury Duty (1995)
Captive (1995)
A Modern Affair (1995)
It Could Happen to You (1994)
Mrs. Parker and the Vicious Circle (1994)
Somebody to Love (1994)
The Pelican Brief (1993)
Undercover Blues (1993)
The Public Eye (1992)
In the Soup (1992)
Beethoven (1992)
Prelude to a Kiss (1992)
Billy Bathgate (1991)
Men of Respect (1991)
Quick Change (1990)
Slaves of New York (1989)
Fear, Anxiety & Depression (1989)
The Feud (1989)
Monkey Shines: An Experiment in Fear (1988)
Who's That Girl? (1987)
Prizzi's Honor (1985)

Director

Joe Gould's Secret (1999)
The Impostors (1998)
Big Night (1996)

Acknowledgements

"Gianni Amelio..." was published in the *Globe & Mail*, October 1995.

"Dario Argento..." was published in *Tandem Magazine*, August 1996.

"Bertolucci 1..." was published in *Scene Magazine,* June 1994.

"Bertolucci 2..." was published in *Tandem Magazine,* June 1996.

"Franco Brusati..." was published in *Showtimes Magazine,* March 1991.

"Steve Buscemi..." was published in *Tandem Magazine,* October 1996.

"Mimmo Calopresti..." was published in *Tandem Magazine,* March 1997.

"Michael Corrente..." was published in *Tandem Magazine,* September 1996.

"Don Coscarelli..." was published in *Tandem Magazine,* August 1998.

"Tom DiCillo..." was published in *Tandem Magazine,* October 1997.

"Richard LaGravanese..." was published in *Tandem Magazine,* October 1998.

"Anthony Mainghella..." was published in *Tandem Magazine,* November 1996.

"Nanni Moretti..." was published in the *Globe & Mail,* September 1993.

"Greg Mottola..." was published in *Tandem Magazine,* March 1997.

"Maurizio Nichetti..." was published in *Tandem Magazine,* August 1996.

"Al Pacino..." was published in *Scene Magazine,* October 1996.

"Leone Pompucci..." was published in *Tandem Magazine,* March 1996.

"Gabriele Salvatores..." was published in *eye Weekly* magazine October, 1991.

"Michele Soavi..." was published in *Tandem Magazine,* May 1996.

"Giuseppe Tornatore..." was published in the *Toronto Star,* July 1991.

"Stanley Tucci..." was published in *Tandem Magazine,* September 1996.

Printed in June 1999 by
VEILLEUX
ON DEMAND PRINTING INC.

in Longueuil, Quebec